Pub Walks in Oxfordshire

Laurence Main

Published by Sigma Leisure – an imprint of
Sigma Press, 1 South Oak Lane, Wilmslow, Cheshire SK9 6AR, England.

Whilst every effort has been made to ensure that the information given in this book is correct, neither the publisher nor the author accept any responsibility for any inaccuracy.

British Library Cataloguing in Publication Data
A CIP record for this book is available from the British Library.

ISBN: 1-85058-302-1

Typesetting and Design by: Sigma Press, Wilmslow, Cheshire.

Maps by: Morag Perrott

Text photographs: by the author

Cover photograph: The Angel, Henley-on-Thames

Printed and bound by
Manchester Free Press, Paragon Mill, Jersey St., Manchester M4 6FP.

Preface

Oxfordshire is a fascinating countryside for walking. It lacks the rugged character of further north or west, but this doesn't detract from its variety and sense of tranquillity. Despite the car factories at Cowley, agriculture still reigns supreme. The Romans farmed here and left traces of their villas. Some sites date back to the New Stone Age, when prehistoric tracks such as the Ridgeway were of national importance. The county boundary changes of 1974 gave Oxfordshire extra acres and some fine paths through ancient landscapes.

Visitors to the area would do well to base themselves in Oxford. This 'city of dreaming spires' is where the druids located the 'navel of Britain'. It is a place for contemplation and the natural home for our senior university. The architecture that Hitler didn't want to bomb belongs to the world, and during a long tourist season it does seem as if the whole world has come to admire it. Many come to learn the language as it should be spoken. Few foreigners appreciate that there is only one way to explore Oxford . . . on foot. A set of 'On Foot in Oxford' guides is available from Oxford Library and should keep the newcomer occupied for at least a week without stepping into the countryside. Not that the countryside ever feels far away in a city that can boast Christchurch Meadows, the University Parks, the towpath of the River Thames and much else. Oxford is special. I remember applying in person for a visa to enter Afghanistan when in Meshed, eastern Iran. The whimsical official dallied disdainfully with other applicants from places like Enfield, York and Manchester. Then he asked where I came from. 'Ah Oxford', he said with a gleam in his eye. My passport was stamped and I entered Afghanistan well before the others.

Oxford is the hub at the centre of the county's public transport system. Bus routes radiate from it. Unfortunately, deregulation has brought the evils of competition. Where is the benefit to the passenger in having rival companies that don't accept each other's tickets and don't publicise or co-ordinate their rival timetables? If you travel from Oxford to Witney, for instance, you'll have to decide in advance if your day return ticket is to be bought on a blue bus or a red bus. This will inevitably mean that you have to wait at the bus stop in Witney at the end of the walk and watch blue buses depart for Oxford while your day return ticket is only valid on red buses. Planning day rover bus trips is also complicated by having to stick to a single company's territory each day.

Nevertheless, buses do provide ramblers in Oxfordshire with useful means of access to the start of many a good walk. Public transport details for each walk are detailed within this book. The principal operators are Oxford Bus Company (0865 711312), Thames Transit (0865 727000) and Midland Red South (0295 262368). There are other, obscure, bus companies with the most exotic of routes. If in doubt, contact Oxfordshire County Council, Public Transport Section, Department of Planning and Property Services, Speedwell House, Speedwell Street, Oxford, OX1 1SD, Tel. 0865 810405.

Life becomes easier when you patronise good old British Rail (if it is still allowed to exist). Let the train take the strain north to Banbury, calling at places like Heyford. The line to Bicester has been reopened and Islip station is proving to be a Mecca for ramblers (it serves both the Oxfordshire Way and the Oxfordshire Trek). The Cotswold Line towards Worcester via Charlbury is another really useful railway, while the train comes into its own on the line down the Thames Valley from Oxford via Didcot towards Reading and London Paddington. There is a branch line to Henley, but this is easier to reach by bus. Riverboats can take you to Abingdon (contact Salter Bros Ltd. on 0865 243421).

Oxford has to cater for tourists, so there is plenty of all types of accommodation. Book in advance, however, especially if you intend staying at Oxford's youth hostel. There is a camp-site at Camping International on the southern edge of Oxford near a bus stop for frequent services along the Abingdon Road into the city, or south to Abingdon and Wantage in the other direction. Tourist information is available from Oxford Information Centre, St. Aldate's, Oxford, OX1

1DY, Tel. 0865 726871. There are Tourist Information Centres in Abingdon, Banbury, Burford, Chipping Norton, Cropredy, Faringdon, Henley, Oxford, Thame, Wallingford, Witney and Woodstock.

Oxfordshire used to lag behind neighbouring counties (especially Gloucestershire) in the matter of waymarking and maintenance of public footpaths. That is no longer the case. Returning to the county at regular intervals since leaving Oxford with one of its university's degrees in 1973, I can testify to a steady improvement. Now when you plan a route from an Ordnance Survey Pathfinder map, you can be pretty sure that it will be easy to follow on the ground. This book is designed to give you the necessary experience to acquire the confidence to go out and do just that.

Laurence Main

CONTENTS

Introduction	1
Long Distance Paths	4
Real Ale	6
Location Map	10 & 11

The Walks

Location	*Distance*	*Pub*	
1. Broughton Castle	7 miles	Woolpack Inn	12
2. Adderbury	6 miles	Plough Inn	18
3. Juniper Hill	6 miles	Fox Inn	23
4. Chastleton	6^1/$_2$ miles	Cross Hands Inn	28
5. Enstone	5^1/$_2$ miles	Bell Inn	34
6. Heyford	5 miles	Bell Inn	39
7. Woodstock	10 miles	Marlborough Arms	44
8. Otmoor	6 miles	Red Lion Inn	50
9. Asthall	7 miles	White Hart Inn	55

Location	Distance	Pub	
10. Witney	7^1/$_2$ miles	Cross Keys Inn	60
11. Cumnor	5 miles	Vine Inn	66
12. Godstow	6 miles	Trout Inn	71
13. Garsington	4 miles	Plough Inn	76
14. Thame	7 miles	Black Horse	81
15. Coleshill	6 miles	Radnor Arms	85
16. Faringdon	6 miles	Bell Hotel	90
17. Abingdon	6^1/$_2$ miles	King's Head and Bell	94
18. Dorchester	7 miles	Fleur De Lys	100
19. Christmas Common	5 miles	Carvers' Arms	107
20. Wantage	10 miles	Bell Inn	111
21. Blewbury	9 miles	Red Lion Inn	116
22. Wallingford	10 miles	George Hotel	122
23. Stonor	6 miles	Rainbow Inn	128
24. Uffington White Horse	7^1/$_2$ miles	Rose and Crown	133
25. The Maharajah's Well	6 miles	Cherry Tree Inn	141
26. Henley-on-Thames	7 miles	Angel on the Bridge	146
27. Mapledurham	8 miles	Ferry Boat Inn	151

Introduction

Where does Oxfordshire belong? It is within commuting distance of
London but far enough away to resist inclusion in the South-East.
Wessex has historical claims to the south of the county, while the
Cotswolds extend over its western side. The North Oxfordshire Plain
leads to Banbury, but this town looks more to the industrial Midlands
than to Oxford. The whole of the county is drained by the River Thames
and its tributaries. The County that Edward the Elder laid out in 911-12
(and gained a slice of Berkshire with the local government changes in
1974) stands on its own surrounded by contrasting influences. Easy to
reach from many urban areas, the Oxfordshire countryside offers a
hotchpotch of scenery. There are no mountains, but there are excellent
footpaths which won't overtire the walker.

The limestone and ironstone hills of the Cotswolds in the west and
north-west are sheep country. The local stone adds character and the
villages blend in with the surroundings. There are streams and rivers,
which are absent in the chalk hills of the Chilterns, on the opposite side
of the county. Glorious beech trees give shelter to wildlife and carpets of
bluebells in the spring. North of the unique city of Oxford, the rich soil
of the Oxfordshire Plain is studded with villages built of honey-coloured
stone. Racehorses now canter where our prehistoric ancestors roamed
the Downs and the Vale of White Horse. The River Isis flows through
Oxford to join the River Thame at Dorchester and form the Thames
Valley, now the home of stockbrokers as London comes nearer. Oxford
has no reason to bow to London, however. Twice it was the capital of
England (during the Civil War and the Plague) and Hitler wanted to
make it his capital.

The gravels of the Thames valley suited the primitive ploughs of the neolithic farmers who came here in about 4000 BC. Abingdon produced pottery around 2500 BC. It is to the hills that we should look for dramatic evidence of our distant ancestors, however. Wayland's Smithy is a particularly significant spot near the White Horse of Uffington.

Oxfordshire is rich in the enigmatic cursus structures which can be seen at Dorchester and are known through aerial photography in many other places. The Rollright Stones guard the border with Warwickshire and would appear to be on a ley line with Banbury Cross by way of St. Mary's Church, Broughton.

In the Iron Age, from about 500 BC, the upper Thames was a frontier zone. The Dobunni held the west and the Belgic Catuvellauni came to the east. Neither offered much resistance to the Romans. The prominent earthwork known as Grim's Ditch could antedate or postdate the Romans, who built Akeman Street to connect St. Alban's and Cirencester. A Roman town was built at Alchester, near Bicester, where a road from Silchester via Dorchester met Akeman Street. The town didn't survive the Roman withdrawal, unlike the ancient British settlement of Dorchester, which was continuously occupied and became the first bishopric of Wessex.

Oxfordshire is thought of as being Saxon, with the legendary Hengist thrusting up the Thames Valley to Hinksey, near Oxford. It suffered from being fought over by Wessex and Mercia and later by Saxons and Danes. It was the need to secure the Thames that led King Alfred the Great (who was born at Wantage) to invest in Oxford, although Wallingford was considered more important. Both places figured in the civil war fought between Matilda and Stephen after the Norman Conquest.

There isn't much wilderness left in Oxfordshire, but there is a lot of agricultural land. Oilseed rape adds its yellow colour to the spring landscape, much of which is owned by Oxford colleges. The rich became richer and the poor became poorer as the land was enclosed in the late 18th and 19th centuries. Farm labourers could no longer graze their animals on common pasture. Flora Thompson recorded in *Lark Rise to Candleford* how 'Country people had not been poor when Sally was a girl, or their prospects as hopeless. Sally's father had kept a cow, geese, poultry, pigs and a donkey-cart to carry his produce to the market town. He could do this because he had commoners' rights and could turn his animals out to graze, and cut furze for firing and even turf to make a lawn for one of his customers'.

The richest farms were in the south-east near Goring and Ewelme, where wheat, roots, greens, oats, barley, beans and clover were grown. Garsington was in an area where market gardens flourished by supplying Oxford. Dairying was the feature of the Vale of White Horse, with the Great Western Railway becoming known as the Milky Way. The rich soils of the north weren't as well provided with transport, so butter was sent to the Birmingham market. Banbury was famous for its cheeses as well as its cakes.

Wheat is the most important Oxfordshire crop, with barley grown mostly west of the River Cherwell. Stoke Row was once famous for its cherry orchards, while Letcombe Bassett was named Cresscombe by Thomas Hardy in *Jude the Obscure.*

Witney blankets testify to the high quality of wool from Cotswold sheep. The Indians of Virginia and New England traded furs for Witney blankets in the 17th century. Earlys of Witney won a 1000 guinea wager on 8th June, 1906, by shearing sheep, weaving their wool into cloth and making a coat from it in just 10 hours and 27 minutes.

Woodstock makes high quality gloves for aristocrats. Further north, at Hook Norton, the Brymbo Iron Works was established in 1896. The. Oxfordshire Ironstone Company operated in the area west of Banbury until 1967. No wonder this area was famous for its beer!

The University has been a major employer in Oxford for centuries and printing is its natural companion. Motor cars spread Oxford's name around the globe in the 20th century, however, as a result of William Morris setting himself up in business here shortly after leaving school in Cowley at 16. Atomic energy research is established at Harwell and Culham, while Banbury has maintained its reputation for food by becoming the U.K. Head Office of General Foods (incorporating Bird's).

The River Thames made Oxford a commercial centre. By 1790, the Oxford Canal had added a connection to the industrial Midlands. As the railways took away the goods trade, so the pleasure-boaters arrived, including Jerome K. Jerome's *Three Men in a Boat*. Oxford won the first boat race over Cambridge in 1829 and the Eights still stir enthusiasm at the end of May in Oxford. Henley's famous Regatta is in early July.

Oxfordshire is rich in country houses. Broughton Castle was the home of William Fiennes, who conspired against Charles I. There were no Puritans at Stonor Park, where the Stonors paid heavily for keeping their Roman Catholic faith. Minster Lovell had a secret room too, for Lord Lovell to hide (and perish) in after the Battle of Stoke in 1487.

Thame Park incorporates part of the medieval Cistercian abbey. Mapledurham has a fine example of a Tudor house, while Chastleton house is Jacobean and built from the wealth of Cotswold wool. Rousham House was a generation later, then remodelled in Gothic style in 1738-40 by William Kent. The gardens give a romantic, naturalistic effect, in the Italian manner.

All these are but a prelude to the splendour of Blenheim Palace, near Woodstock. The nation's tribute to John Churchill, Duke of Marlborough, became the birthplace of Sir Winston Churchill. Don't leave Oxfordshire without visiting it. One place you won't be allowed to see is Friar Park, Henley. Built as a folly in 1896, the grounds include a maze, caves and underground lakes lit by electricity to show artificial monsters and spiders. It is now the home of the ex-Beatle George Harrison.

Long Distance Paths

Oxfordshire is criss-crossed by long distance paths. 64 to 65 miles is a popular length, allowing the energetic to complete the walk over a Bank Holiday weekend or the leisurely rambler to walk it in a week. *The Oxfordshire Way* is a 65 mile route from Bourton-on-the-Water in Gloucestershire to Henley-on-Thames. It thus links two Areas of Outstanding Natural Beauty, the Cotswolds and the Chilterns. It also links the Heart of England Way with the Thames Walk. Devised by members of the Oxfordshire branch of the Council for the Protection of

Rural England, superbly-drawn route maps were published in 1975. The first edition of the guidebook followed in 1978.

A year later, in 1979, *The Oxfordshire Trek* was self-published by Laurence Main. A second edition was published in 1989 by Kittiwake Press. This 64 mile route encircles Oxford and is designed to be easily split into shorter day sections with the aid of public transport radiating from the city. It starts and finishes at Sir Winston Churchill's tomb at Bladon, passes Blenheim Palace and Dorchester Abbey, as well as George Orwell's grave at Sutton Courtenay.

Also 64 miles long is *The d'Arcy Dalton Way*. This route was published in 1985 to mark the Ramblers' Association's Golden Jubilee. The late Col. W. P. d'Arcy Dalton gave over 50 years service in the cause of rights of way in Oxfordshire. It starts on the Oxford Canal, just over the border in Warwickshire, passes Hook Norton, the Rollrights and finishes at Wayland's Smithy.

This brings us to the Oldest Road, the famous *Ridgeway*. Part of this ancient track is now a National Trail, from Overton Hill near Avebury, in Wiltshire, to Ivinghoe Beacon, in Buckinghamshire. Some 85 or 89 miles long (take your pick from various guidebooks), this is an exceptionally interesting route for anybody who likes history. Uffington White Horse and Wayland's Smithy are the prime sites, but hillforts include Uffington Castle and Letcombe Castle or Segsbury Camp.

King Alfred's Way crosses the Ridgeway above Wantage, where King Alfred was born in 849. This 108 mile route was pioneered by Laurence Main in 1979 and his guidebook was published by Thornhill Press in 1980. It starts at H.M.S. Victory in Portsmouth and soon follows an Alfred Road. Alfred's capital at Winchester is visited while the finish is in Oxford, the home of Alfred's Jewel (in the Ashmolean Museum).

Another National Trail will soon go through Oxford. *The Thames Walk* has been advocated since the National Parks and Access to the Countryside Act of 1949. The loss of many ferries meant a continuous walking route was lost when the towpath switched banks (hence the delay in establishing this route). David Sharp's guidebook to the 175 mile journey from the Thames Barrier at Greenwich to the source near Kemble is published by the Ramblers' Association.

Real Ale

Oxfordshire has plenty of malting barley and brewing was one of the county's major industries. In the Middle Ages, ale was drunk by virtually everybody because it was safer then water, having been boiled and containing preservatives. Unlike modern beer, it was thick, sticky and sweet and might have included exotic spices. Hopped beer wasn't introduced, from Flanders, until the 14th century. It was thought fit only to be drunk by Dutchmen and Henry VIII forbade his brewers to add hops. By the late 16th century, however, nearly all ales contained hops in order to keep better. This was when less people made their own ale and licensed brewers were becoming common. There were close links between baking and brewing, especially in Banbury.

Most people in the countryside continued to brew their own beer until higher taxes were imposed and fuel became scarce with the enclosure of the 19th century. Beer became the drink of the pub around 1800, while tea was now drunk at home. Home-brewing wasn't to revive until commercially-made kits appeared in the 1970s. Large scale brewing had previously been the province of the great monastic houses. Abingdon Abbey had an active brewhouse and malthouse. Some Oxford colleges also built their own brewhouses, with Merton College's recorded in 1284. Queen's College maintained its brewery from 1340-41 until 1939.

The authorities liked the idea of professional brewers, because it made control and taxation easier. The addition of hops allowed longer storage and wider distribution and enabled a few large-scale brewers to concentrate production in their hands.

Morland's of Abingdon has survived as a brewery that began in West Ilsley on the Berkshire Downs in 1711. The family acquired the Eagle Brewery in Abingdon in 1866 and transferred activities to it. The present brewery was built on its site in 1911-12. Amalgamations secured nearly 300 tied public houses in the early 20th century. Old Speckled Hen was brewed especially for the MG Jubilee in 1979.

Brakspear's Henley Brewery is famous for its real ale. Robert Brakspear took over his uncle (Richard Hayward's) brewery in Henley in 1803. By improving the beers and taking over more tied houses, he caused the business to grow. In 1896 Brakspear's bought out their last local rival and has managed to retain its independence and flourish in the 20th century. You'll find its range of beers all over South Oxfordshire.

The Hook Norton Brewery is also proud of its independence, having adapted to meet changing times since John Harris established himself as a maltster in 1847. Beer was being brewed commercially by 1856, all to freehouses. One tied house, in Hook Norton, was purchased in 1869. Now it has 34 tied houses and has a big demand from freehouses. A lifeline was the securing of a Government licence to supply Coventry Working Men's Clubs since 1918. Look out for Old Hookey in places up to fifty miles from Hook Norton.

Mark and James Morrell, father and son, married into the brewing business in Oxford in the late 18th century. An old site was used in St. Thomas' and by 1896 it was capable of producing 2500 barrels a week. Still independent, Morrell's owns 140 pubs in the Oxford area. The family became very prosperous. Philip Morrell, M.P. for South Oxfordshire, and his wife, Lady Ottoline, often entertained famous literary figures at Garsington Manor (see route 13).

Hall's Brewery is another old Oxford institution, dating from 1795, when William Hall purchased the Swan's Nest Brewery. Take-overs brought tied houses and these were supplied by a fleet of over 60 brewery drays. These formed a procession around Oxford on May Day before the First World War. bulk orders were also sent by river, although the coming of the railway to Oxford in 1851 was a significant date. Taken over by Alsops in 1926, it became part of Ind Coope, now part of Allied Breweries. Allied were persuaded to establish Hall's Oxford and West Brewery Company Ltd. in 1980 in order to meet the revival of consumer interest in traditional ales. The beer sold under the Halls trade mark is brewed in Burton. Four beers are brewed on the premises of the Old Red Lion in Oxford's Gloucester Green, however. Ask for *Tapper* and *Oxbow*.

Opening Hours

Under recent legislation pubs in England can now open for a maximum of 12 hours each day on Mondays to Saturdays (being 11am to 11pm) and for six and a half hours on Sundays (12 noon to 3pm and 7pm to

10.30pm) unless extensions have been granted by local licensing
magistrates. Additionally, a growing number of pubs stay open during
Sunday afternoons to serve meals, with which alcohol may then be
consumed on the premises.

Most country pubs do not find it in their interest to take full advantage
of these 'relaxed' hours and tend to stick to the 'traditional' hours of 12
noon to 3 pm and 6pm to 11pm or 7pm to 11pm. Check each pub
individually.

The Walks

Each of the walks in this book follows rights of way to which you, as a
member of the public, has unrestricted access. These are public
footpaths, bridleways and by-ways as well as lanes and roads. When
surveyed, all these routes were free of obstructions. Such a statement is a
tribute to the work of the Oxfordshire Area of the Ramblers' Association
and to the County Council's Rights of Way officers. Should you discover
any problems on rights of way in Oxford, send full details (including
grid references) to the Ramblers' Association at 1/5 Wandsworth Road,
London, SW8 2XX, and to the Rights of Way Officer, Oxfordshire County
Council, Department of Leisure and Arts, Central Library, Westgate,
Oxford, OX1 1DJ (Tel. 0865 810808).

The walks are numbered in sequence from north to south and are spread
all over Oxfordshire. Make use of the Ordnance Survey Pathfinder maps,
details of which are given for each walk. These are beautiful keys to the
countryside which all walkers should become familiar with. Studying
them will show where certain walks can be linked together should a
longer route be desired or access to a bus stop be necessary. Walks 26
(Henley-on-Thames) and 23 (Stonor) meet at the Rainbow Inn, Middle
Assendon, to give a 13 mile walk. Walks 9 (Asthall) and 10 (Witney)
connect at the White Hart Inn, Minster Lovell, to give a $14^1/_2$ mile walk.
Walks 15 (Coleshill) and 16 (Faringdon) join at Great Coxwell to give a

12 mile walk. Walks 22 (Wallingford) and 25 (The Maharajah's Well) can be combined by a short stretch of road to form a route of over 17 miles.

All walks should be within the capabilities of anyone of average fitness. Allow about one hour for every two miles, which should enable short breaks to be made. Do remember that the physical landscape is changing all the time, for example as hedgerows are grubbed up and fields amalgamated. Keep to the path and always regard it as a privilege to walk across someone else's land; in that way we can build an atmosphere of co-operation, rather than confrontation, in the country-side.

The Country Code

❑ Guard against all risk of fire.

❑ Fasten all gates.

❑ Keep dogs under proper control.

❑ Avoid damaging fences, hedges and walls.

❑ Keep to paths across farmland.

❑ Leave no litter.

❑ Safeguard water supplies.

❑ Protect wildlife, wild plants and trees.

❑ Go carefully on country roads.

❑ Respect the life of the countryside.

LOCATION MAP

Northamptonshire

N

3 Juniper Hill

5 miles

Heyford
6
BICESTER

SHIRE

Otmoor
8

Buckinghamshire

12 Godstow   14 THAME
OXFORD   13 Garsington

ABINGDON
17   Dorchester   19 Christmas Common
18

DIDCOT   WALLINGFORD   23 Stonor
22

21   The
Blewbury   Maharajah's
Well 25   26
HENLEY-ON-THAMES

27 Mapledurham

1. *Broughton Castle*

Route: The Woolpack Inn, Banbury – Crouch Hill – Wykham Lane – Broughton Castle – Giant's Cave – Salt Way – Banbury Cross – The Woolpack Inn, Banbury.

Distance: 7 miles.

Maps: O.S. Pathfinders 1022 Banbury (North) and 1045 Brackley and Banbury (South).

Start: The Woolpack Inn, Banbury (Grid Reference SP 453405).

Access: Banbury is easy to reach by train, being on the main line between Oxford and Birmingham. Lots of buses radiate from its bus station, while there are local trains to Bicester and the Chilterns. Car parks are signed.

The Woolpack Inn, Banbury (0295 262915)

Its name refers to the old packhorse trade routes which met here. This old building looks out on Horse Fair, where sheep were sold on one side of the street and horses on the other. Records show the pub wasn't established until 1846, however. Long before then, it seems that a nunnery was housed here. This is an example of how Banbury can swing to extremes. Discuss this with the locals as you sup real ale and eat a bar snack. The pub can also offer bed and breakfast accommodation (but no ghostly nuns). Opening hours are 11 am to 3 pm and 5 pm to 11 pm on weekdays, 12 noon to 3 pm and 7 pm to 10.30 pm on Sundays.

The Nursery Rhyme Way

> *'Ride-a-cock-horse to Banbury Cross,*
> *To see a fine lady on a white horse.*
> *With rings on her fingers and bells on here toes,*
> *She shall have music wherever she goes.'*

We have here a Celtic goddess, Rhiannon, riding her white horse to celebrate Beltane (May Day). Feasts demand cakes and Banbury is famous for these too. Great truths are hidden in nursery rhymes and while Banbury may appear as an outpost of the Midlands and, as the second largest town in Oxfordshire, a major centre in its own right, its identity is only revealed to little children.

Is this a similar spot to Wittenham Clumps, overlooking Dorchester (see route 18), where male and female energy lines cross? If so, it would help to explain the intensity of feelings, like spiritual possession, here as one or other energy gains dominance. Although the town dates from early Saxon times, nearby Crouch Hill was the scene of Celtic May Day revels. It is from their May Queen that Banbury became famous throughout the English speaking world.

Contrast this with the rise of Puritanism in the town. Around 1600, they destroyed the Maypole and the town's three crosses. The present Banbury Cross dates from 1858, but it is on a straight line between two of its predecessors, the old White Cross (in West Bar) and the old Bread Cross (in Butchers Row). This direct line is significant.

Two prehistoric trackways cross at Giant's Cave, between Banbury and Broughton. The Salt Way was used to carry salt from Droitwich to London, while the Jurassic Way went north-eastwards from the Rollright Stones. There is a big pit near the junction now which is reputedly a filled-in tunnel which linked this spot with Broughton Castle, one mile away.

Tunnel legends (often with token lengths of tunnel dug) can be folk memories of leys. Here I record a personal discovery. Sheltering from the rain in the church at Broughton (and re-writing my sodden notes before they disintegrated), I met a farmer on a visit with a National Trust Group from a neighbouring county. It transpired that he had two genuine crop circles on his land and his wife (a seventh daughter of a seventh daughter) had taken him to John Michell's Crop Circle Conference in Glastonbury in 1991. I told him of the tunnel legend and we decided to dowse for a ley. We both dowsed the same ley and then opened the maps to plot its route from our compass bearing. No, it didn't go to the Giant's Cave. It went between it and Crouch Hill (could these be visited by spiralling male and female energy lines?) straight through the site of the old White Cross, the present Banbury Cross and the old Bread Cross.

We then drew the line in the other direction and it led straight to . . . the King Stone, Rollright! We were both strangers to the area and had no idea of the direction we were dowsing and I, at least, had expected a line to the Giant's Cave without having studied the map for any alignments. Why not try dowsing around St. Mary's Church, Broughton, for yourself (the ley cuts across a corner of Broughton Castle's moat)?

Broughton Castle came by marriage to the Fiennes family in 1451 and it's still theirs. The family were keen Puritans and important meetings were held here before and during the Civil War. Visits can be made on Wednesdays and Sundays from mid May to Mid September, plus Thursdays in July and August, also Bank Holiday Sundays and Bank Holiday Mondays (including Easter), all between 2 pm and 5 pm. Telephone 0295 262624 for latest details.

Broughton Castle

The Fiennes Family had many Puritan supporters in Banbury. The town once known for its May Queen became notorious for its inhabitant seen 'A hanging his cat on Monday for killing a mouse on Sunday'. There is much more history here and the Banbury Museum, near the end of this walk (open April to September, Monday to Saturday, 10 am to 5 pm and October to March, Tuesday to Saturday, 10 am to 4.30 pm, admission free) is the place to learn all about it. Sit down to watch the introductory video on 'Banburyshire'. Remember, you read about the ley running from the King Stone, Rollright, through St. Mary's Church, Broughton, to Banbury Cross here first!

The Walk

1. Cross the road (Horse Fair) outside the Woolpack Inn. Pass Banbury Cross on your left. Go right up West Bar Street. Bear right up Broughton Road to a roundabout. Turn left along Queen's Way.

2. Turn right along Brantwood Rise. Go left at Browning Road, then turn right along Masefield Road. Turn left at Brooke Road. At its junction with Byron Road, take the narrow footpath ahead between houses Nos. 17 and 19.

3. Follow the field path past the tree-clad summit of Crouch Hill on your right. Go through a gap in the middle of the hedge ahead, level with the last of the trees on your right. Bear left to a narrow gap in the hedge on your left. Take care to find this about 150 yards from the near corner of this field on your left.

4. Go through the gap in the hedge to cross Salt Way (a track) and take a gap in the hedge immediately opposite. Although both gaps in the two hedges are narrow and hard to find, they lead to a field path which is obvious. Follow this across the field, bearing slightly right to a gate in the far corner. Continue past Crouch Farm on your right, cross its concrete access lane and walk with a hedge on your right.

5. Turn right through a gate in the corner and follow a hedge on your left for 30 yards, then turn left through a gap in it. Turn right immediately to walk with the hedge now on your right. Reach a corner,

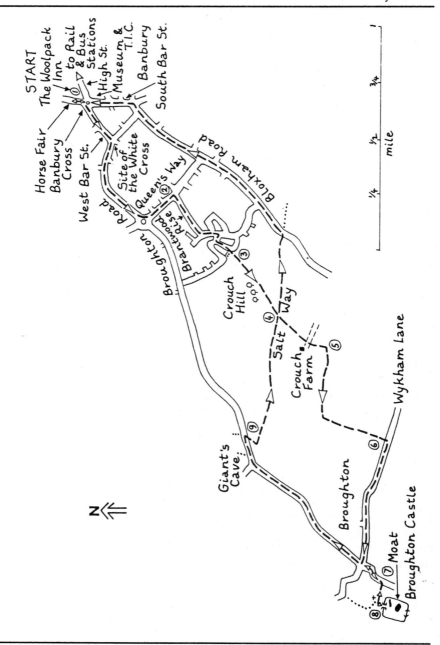

where the right of way goes ahead to the next field. You can achieve this by taking a narrow gap in the hedge (a little to the left of the corner). Turn left to follow the hedge on your left to a road (Wykham Lane).

6. Turn right along Wykham Lane to Broughton. Reach a crossroads and turn left to pass the Saye and Sele Arms pub on your right (temporarily vacant when I called). Follow the pavement until it ends.

7. Turn right along the paved path to St. Mary's Church. Go through the churchyard, passing the church on your right, and turn left for Broughton Castle.

8. Retrace your steps to the crossroads at Broughton. Go ahead along the road to Banbury. Pass a road on your left, then reach a signposted footpath on your left. Divert along it briefly to see the pit that remains of the Giant's Cave. Return to the road and resume walking towards Banbury. Come to a wooden staircase on your left that is way-marked as part of the Banbury Fringe Circular Walk.

9. Turn sharply right to follow the ancient track known as the Salt Way. Eventually come to a road (Bloxham Road) and turn left along its pavement into Banbury. Turn left at South Bar Street. Pass Banbury Museum and Tourist Information Centre, just before Banbury Cross. The Woolpack Inn is ahead, in Horse Fair, on your right.

2. *Adderbury*

Route: The Plough Inn, Adderbury – Kemps Farm – Oxford Canal – Nellbridge Lock – Adderbury Lakes – The Plough Inn, Adderbury.

Distance: 6 miles.

Map: O.S. Pathfinder 1045 Brackley and Banbury (South).

Start: The Plough Inn, Adderbury (Grid Reference SP 478358).

Access: Adderbury is three miles south of Banbury, from where there are a number of buses (X59, 491 and 499 run by Midland Red, Tel. 0295 253451, 30 run by Tex Cars, Tel. 0295 738888 and Heyfordian, Tel. 0869 232957). There is a car park at the Plough Inn. The nearest railway station is at King's Sutton, which is served by trains on the Banbury – Oxford line and the Chiltern Line between London Marylebone and Banbury via Bicester North. If you come by train, add a total of three miles to this walk ($1^1/_2$ miles each way) and follow the road to join the circuit at point 5.

The Plough Inn, Adderbury (0295 810327)

Brew XI, Marston's Pedigree and Stone's Bitter are the real ales served here. Come on a Saturday night for live entertainment, although when Norman Wisdom called in it was for a drink rather than a professional engagement. Meals and bar snacks are available. The pub dates from the second half of the 18th century. Opening hours are 11 am to 2.30 pm and 7 pm to 11 pm on weekdays, 12 noon to 3 pm and 7 pm to 10.30 pm on Sundays. Dogs, children and mud are not welcome!

Adderbury

Adderbury House was once the home of the dissolute Earl of Rochester. He lost contact with his father, who followed King Charles II into exile during the Civil War. With his father dying abroad in 1658, two years before the Restoration, he succeeded to the title at the age of 10. His mother pushed him to acquire an education and he gained a Master of Arts degree from Oxford in 1661. Still tender in years, he set off on the Grand Tour of the continent. The Court held no terrors for him when he first appeared, aged 17, in 1664. He soon gained notoriety for kidnapping a beautiful heiress, Elizabeth Mallett. He was thrown into the Tower but eventually regained royal favour and married the girl. His wife paid his bills and was left alone for long spells at Adderbury while the Earl lived a profligate life at court, writing verses which lampooned Charles II and the Kings mistresses. He soon wore his body out and died repentant in 1680. His wife and only son followed him to the grave a year later.

Adderbury Lakes were laid out by Capability Brown, the famous 18th century landscape designer. They are now a haven for wildlife, having been cleared recently by the Manpower Services Commission. Poplar, yew, beech, maple, sycamore, alder, oak, ash and willow trees surround the lakes, while there is even a tulip tree. The range of wild flowers is similarly impressive, while a kingfisher is just one of the feathered residents.

Adderbury Lakes

The Walk

1. With your back to the Plough Inn, go left along the pavement. Pass Keyte's Close on your left and a school on your right. Reach traffic lights at a T junction. Turn right along the pavement of the road to Banbury. Pass a bus stop on your left and The Rise on your right.

2. Turn right up Kemps Road. When this turns left, go straight ahead along a metalled footpath. Maintain this direction across one road and reach a second. Turn left along this road's pavement for 100 yards then, immediately after No. 41 on your right, turn right up a rough lane towards Kemps Farm.

3. Just before Kemps Farm, turn left through a small, black, metal gate. Pass the farmyard on your right, bear right through a gate in a temporary fence and cross a field to the stile beside a gate in the hedge

Nellbridge Lock, on the Oxford Canal

opposite. Continue along the well-trodden path to a stile beside a gate in the far left corner. Go ahead with a hedge on your left towards a motorway. Turn left over a way-marked stile in the next corner and walk above the motorway, on your right, to a road ahead.

4. Turn right to cross the bridge carrying the road over the motorway. Follow the road down to a bridge over the canal. Cross it.

5. Turn left immediately after the bridge to reach the canal towpath. Turn left to follow it under the bridge, keeping the canal on your right. Continue past Kings Sutton Lock and under a bridge. Pass an old railway bridge still spanning the River Cherwell on

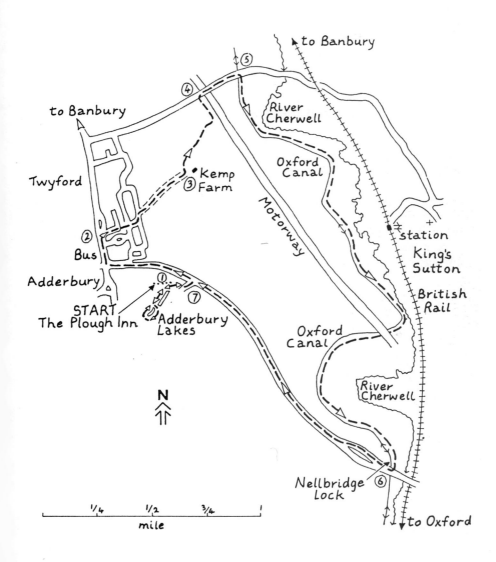

your left but now demolished where it crossed the canal. Follow the towpath under the new motorway bridge. Pass Nellbridge Lock on your right.

6. Turn right over the road bridge after Nellbridge Lock. Fork right to follow the old road which soon rejoins the main road. Continue along its grassy verge towards Adderbury. Pass Banbury Business Park on your right. Cross the road with care to pass the entrance to Bo-peep Farm (a Caravan Club site) and Katharine House Hospice on your left.

7. Turn left to pass East House on your left and go up a No Through Road. Fork right along the metalled footpath which passes a cottage named 'Old Mark's' on your right. Go ahead along Longwall. Soon reach a wooden gate in the wall on your left. Bear left through this to visit Adderbury Lakes and Gardens. Follow the path past the upper lake on your left. Go left over a footbridge at a sluice to walk around the lower lake on your right. Retrace your steps to Longwall and bear right back to the main road. Turn left along the pavement to reach the Plough Inn on your left.

3. *Juniper Hill*

Route: The Fox Inn, Juniper Hill – Larkrise – Cottisford – Tusmore House – Cottisford – The Fox Inn, Juniper Hill.

Distance: 6 miles.

Map: O.S. Pathfinder 1045 Brackley and Banbury (South).

Start: The Fox Inn, Juniper Hill (Grid Reference SP 579325).

Access: Juniper Hill is just off the A42 between Oxford and Northampton. This road is taken by the X38 bus between Oxford and Northampton (Tel. 0604 36681 for timetable information). The authorities don't want this remote hamlet to enjoy the benefits of public transport, however. The bus passes by without being allowed to stop. Would it be that difficult to provide a bus stop? The nearest official bus stop is three miles north along the A42 at Brackley. Bus drivers do, unofficially, drop you at the turning for Juniper Hill and may, more reluctantly, stop to pick up passengers who give vigorous hand signals. Expect a lecture about this not being an official bus stop, however.

The Fox Inn, Juniper Hill (0869 810616)

Hook Norton real ales are served in this pub, which is named the 'Wagon and Horses' in Flora Thompson's autobiographical trilogy 'Lark Rise to Candleford'. This also served as the hamlet's shop in the 19th century. Bar snacks are available and there is a car park for patrons. Opening hours are 12 noon to 2 pm and 7 pm to 11 pm on weekdays, 12 noon to 3 pm and 7 pm to 10.30 pm on Sundays.

Lark Rise to Candleford

This walk covers ground familiar to Laura, the heroine of Flora Thompson's novels 'Lark Rise' (1939), 'Over to Candleford' (1941) and 'Candleford Green' (1943). They were re-issued as one volume entitled 'Lark Rise to Candleford' in 1945, while a fourth book, 'Still glides the stream', was published one year after Flora's death in 1947. Flora was born in 1876 at the cottage now known as Larkrise but originally named Watford Tunnel Cottage, Juniper Hill. Its literary name is 'The End House'. The cottage of Queenie Massey, lacemaker and bee-mistress, stands nearby. She wrote about real people and real places, so their names had to be disguised. Cottisford became 'Fordlow' Fringford (where Flora worked for eight years as a post-mistress) became 'Candleford Green' and Juniper Hill was 'Larkrise'. Flora used to follow the footpath to school at Cottisford during the summer, taking the road in winter.

The trilogy is essential reading for those interested in Oxfordshire, its people and history. Above all, her books contrast the modern era with the recent past. 'Spiritually, they had lost ground, rather than gained it. Their working-class forefathers had religious or political ideals; their talk had not lost the raciness of the soil and was seasoned with native wit which, if sometimes crude, was authentic'. Flora was to marry and move away, but thanks to her writings, we can take 'the path between trees where she had seen the birds' footprints on the snow' and pass 'the pond where the yellow brandyball water-lilies grew'. Like Flora's books, this web of paths is 'spun of love and kinship and cherished memories'.

The Walk

1. With your back to the Fox, go right and turn right immediately along the track through the hamlet of Juniper Hill. Pass allotments on your left and turn right to pass Queenie's cottage on your left. Larkrise is the little white cottage set back just after this. Continue to return to the road.

2. Turn right to pass the Fox on your right, but this time follow the road for 150 yards. Turn right along the signposted public footpath. Follow the track past allotments on your right. Go ahead over a stile in the hedge and bear left diagonally across a field.

3. Take the path through woodland on your left in the corner of this field. Emerge in the corner of another field and go ahead along its edge, with woodland on your right. Take the gap in a hedge ahead to continue to reach the road opposite Duffus House (the old manor house) in Cottisford.

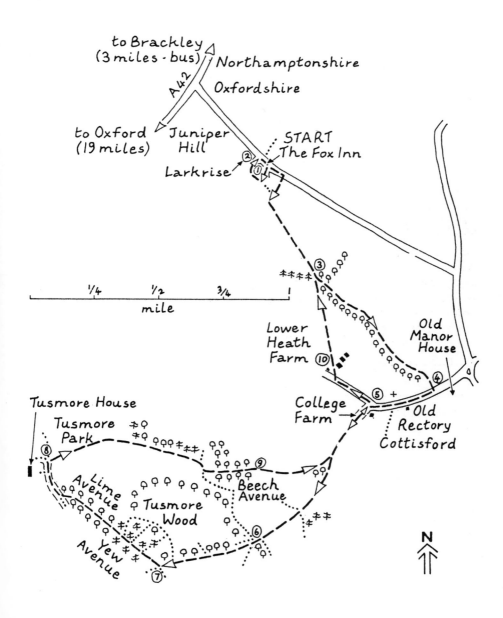

4. Turn right down the road. Pass the old rectory on your left, then St. Mary's Church on your right. Ignore a signposted path going left.

5. When the road bears right, fork left along a concrete farm access lane. This soon deteriorates to a rough, hedged, track after passing College Farm on your left. Continue along the main track, ignoring a path at the start of woodland on your right. Go ahead with the track at a way-marked path crossing. Walk with a hedge on your left and a field on your right.

St Mary's Church, Cottisford

6. Go ahead at a cross-tracks (and ignore the field path bearing left ahead). The track very soon forks. Keep left to pass blackberries and beehives on your right. Continue past a wood, which is carpeted with bluebells in late April and early May, on your right.

7. Turn right down an avenue formed by yew trees. Go ahead through a gate to follow an avenue of lime trees across parkland. Take a gate on your left in the corner. Turn right to follow the drive past Tusmore House on your left.

8. Turn right opposite the entrance to the stables. Go through a gate and cross the parkland, bearing slightly left with the

well-trodden path. Pass a fenced area on your right. Follow the track through a gate in the corner ahead and past woodland on your left. Reach a high deer fence and go right. Turn left along an avenue formed by beech trees.

9. Continue along the edge of a field near the hedge on your left. Pass through a patch of woodland to emerge at your outward track. Turn left to retrace your steps to the road. Go left for 300 yards, then bear right along the signposted footpath which passes the battery hen sheds of Lower Heath Farm on your right.

10. Walk with a hedge on your right. Take the gap ahead to rejoin your outward route. Bear left diagonally across the field to retrace your steps to the pub.

The Fox Inn

4. Chastleton

Route: The Cross Hands Inn, Salford Hill – The Red Lion Inn, Little Compton – Chastleton House – Chastleton Barrow Hillfort – Cornwell – The Cross Hands Inn, Salford Hill.

Distance: 6^1/$_2$ miles.

Maps: O.S. Pathfinders 1044 Moreton-in-Marsh and 1069 Chipping Norton.

Start: The Cross Hands Inn, Salford Hill (Grid Reference SP 270289).

Access: The Cross Hands Inn stands beside the A44 between Chipping Norton and Moreton-in-Marsh at its junction with the A436 from Stow-on-the-Wold. It's less easy to reach by public transport. You have two options, both demanding 3^1/$_2$ miles walking each way (making a full day's walk of 13^1/$_2$ miles, so allow plenty of time). Either take the bus to Chipping Norton (No. 20, 20A, 20B and 20C from Oxford and No. X50 between Oxford and Stratford-upon-Avon) or take British Rail's scenic Cotswold Line between Oxford and Worcester to Moreton-in-Marsh. If you do come by train, start this circuit at point No. 4 (the Red Lion Inn, Little Compton). There is a pavement beside the A44 all the way from Moreton-in-Marsh to Little Compton.

The Cross Hands Inn, Salford Hill (0608 643106)

This very hospitable pub is just inside the Oxfordshire border. It has its own touring caravan and camping site, with beautiful panoramic views over Oxfordshire, Warwickshire and Gloucestershire. This is the Cotswolds and, at about 750 ft. above sea level, the Cross Hands claims to be the highest pub in Oxfordshire. Sir Winston Churchill supped here during World War II, but you'll find no rationing here now. The meals are superb, including cracked wheat and walnuts for vegans. Old Peculiar is just one of the Hook Norton real ales served. Children are welcome and there is a beer garden, plus a car park for patrons. Dating from the 16th century, this was once a highwaymen's pub (hence its name). Now it is open from 11 am to 3 pm and 5.30 pm to 11 pm Mondays to Fridays, 11 am to 11 pm on Saturdays and 12 noon to 3 pm and 7 pm to 10.30 pm on Sundays.

The Cross Hands

The Red Lion Inn, Little Compton (0608 74521)

Bed and breakfast accommodation is available in this 16th century pub, which has a delightful beer garden. Food is available and Donnington's real ales are served. Opening hours are 11 am to 2.30 pm and 6 pm to 11 pm on weekdays, 12 noon to 2 pm and 7 pm to 10.30 pm on Sundays No dogs, please (but there is a play area for children).

Chastleton

Robert Catesby, of Gunpowder Plot fame, sold the estate in 1602. He is said to have spent some of the money on gunpowder for Guy Fawkes. His purchaser was a wealthy woollen merchant from Witney, Walter

Jones. He built a fine Jacobean house which has remained unchanged and is only now moving out of his descendants' hands into the care of the National Trust (who plan to open it to the public in 1993). His grandson, Arthur Jones, fought for King Charles II at the Battle of Worcester in 1651. He fled here after the defeat but was soon followed by Cromwell's soldiers. He hid in a secret room then, while his pursuers slept heavily because his wife had laced their drink with laudanum, he escaped on the best of the Roundheads' horses to another secret place. There was an Iron Age settlement at Chastleton Barrow hillfort. This was usually faced with large blocks of stone. A ley may, characteristically, glance the edge of this ancient earthwork in between the old churches at Chastleton and Cornwell. In fact, this line can be extended to include the churches at Badsey (near Evesham), the significant site of Saintbury and Batsford in Gloucestershire. The Welsh architect Sir Clough Williams-Ellis (of Portmeirion fame) restored Cornwell just before the Second World war for an American lady whose British husband, sadly, didn't survive wartime service with the R.A.F. to live in it.

Chastleton House

The Walk

1. Go down the A44 from the Cross Hands Inn and turn left with the signposted Oxfordshire Cycleway along the minor road towards Rollright. Look for a wooden gate with a bridleway way-mark on your left opposite a small plantation of trees.

2. Turn left through the way-marked gate and go ahead along a bridleway into Warwickshire. Pass a disused quarry on your left. Follow a wall on your right and go straight on downhill to Little Compton.

3. Turn left to walk along the pavement of the road which passes Little Compton on your right. Take the second turning on your right (not counting the access to the old rectory and the glebe lands) for St Denys' Church. Go back to the road and pass the gates of the manor house on your right. Pass a road signposted for Chipping Norton and Oxford on your left. Pass Pool Close on your right, then bear right to the Red Lion Inn, Little Compton.

4. Go back to the road which passes the village. Turn left along the pavement for 10 yards, then turn right across the road to take the signposted path through a small wooden gate. Walk beside a hedge on your left and turn right in the corner of the field to follow a fence on your left to a kissing gate which gives access to the A44.

5. Cross the road to return to Oxfordshire and go ahead up a minor road, passing a school on your left. Ignore a signposted path crossing a stile on your left. Follow the quiet road to a T junction and turn left towards Cornwell. Pass a 'No Through Road' on your right, then Chastleton House on your left.

6. Follow the road past the church of St. Mary the Virgin, on your left. Follow the road as it bends right. Just before it makes a sharp right turn, take the signposted, unfenced, road to Rollright over a cattle grid on your left.

7. Turn right immediately to take the small wooden gate in the corner. Cross the pasture, walking parallel to a wall, then a road (and Gloucestershire) on your right. Go through a metal gate in the fence ahead. Turn left along a farm access lane for 50 yards. Turn right

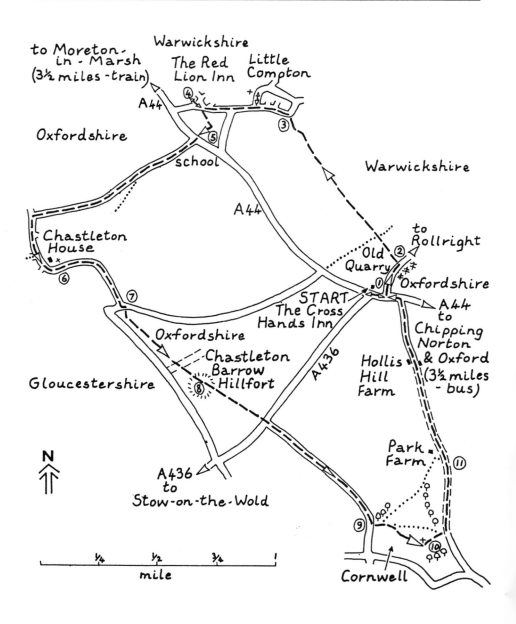

through the second fieldgate on your right. Go ahead beside a fence on your right to the tree-ringed Chastleton Barrow hillfort.

8. Bear slightly left across the interior of the hillfort to a metal gate. Continue beside a hedge on your left to the A436. Cross this road carefully to go ahead along the single track road signposted 'Cornwell only'.

9. When the road bears right, take a signposted path on your left. In fact, three public footpaths go from here. Follow the signed path to the church, soon turning right to reach St. Peter's, Cornwell. Pass this church on your left and take the metal kissing gate out of the far end of the churchyard.

10. Go down parkland. Take a fenced passage ahead, crossing a flat concrete bridge. Climb with a wooden fence on your right to a kissing gate in the top corner. Go through it to a rough lane and turn left along it.

11. Follow the rough lane past a signposted path and Park Farm on your left, then past Hollis Hill Farm. Reach the A44 and turn left (with the signposted Oxfordshire Cycleway). Approach the Cross Hands Inn, on your right.

5. *Enstone*

Route: The Bell Inn, Enstone – Hoar Stone – The Crown Inn, Church Enstone – Cleveley – Radford Bridge – The Bell Inn, Enstone.

Distance: $5^1/_2$ miles.

Maps: O.S. Pathfinders 1068 Chipping Norton & Adlestrop and 1069 Bicester.

Start: The Bell Inn, Enstone (Grid Reference SP 379241).

Access: Enstone is on the A34 five miles south-east of Chipping Norton. The Bell Inn has a car park. There is also a bus stop nearby. This is for the daily service Nos. 20, 20A, 20B and 20C between Oxford and Chipping Norton. Operated by Thames Transit, Tel. 0865 727000 or 0865 772250, this offers four buses each way on Sundays and seven each way on weekdays. The Oxford Bus Company (Tel. 0865 711312 or 0865 774611) offers three buses each way (Nos. X49 and X50) on weekdays between Oxford and Stratford-upon-Avon. Since the infamous decision to deregulate the buses, Oxfordshire has been torn between two competing bus companies who won't accept each other's rover or return tickets and fail to advise passengers of their rival's timetables. In this case, however, the fact that some journeys are subsidised by Oxfordshire County Council means that return tickets are sometimes interchangeable. You still have to go to two different places for two separate timetable leaflets! Whoever caused this chaos (and we all know whom) doesn't actually use public transport.

The Bell Inn, Enstone (0608 677362)

Richard Branson has been known to sup here, but don't let that put you off. This is a friendly 200 year-old pub which serves Fullers real ales – Chiswick, ESB and London Pride. It also does a nice line in bar meals, specialising in Grandma Batty's Yorkshire Pudding. Opening hours are 11.30 am to 3 pm and 6 pm to 11 pm on weekdays, 12 noon to 3 pm and 7 pm to 10.30 pm on Sundays.

The Bell Inn

The Crown Inn, Church Enstone (0608 677262)

Real ale is served here too, along with food. Bed and breakfast accommodation is available and there is a beer garden. This inn is about 250 years old. Opening hours are 12 noon to 3 pm and 7 pm to 11 pm on weekdays, 12 noon to 3 pm and 7 pm to 10.30 pm on Sundays.

Enstone

Five roads join here, giving unity to Church Enstone and Neat Enstone. This was once an important coaching centre, with six inns. This is an ancient route centre, indeed sacred pathways meet here. Two leys cross at the Hoar Stone. Actually a pile of stones, this was originally a burial chamber, erected in Neolithic times. A brief dowsing session around the stones suggested one ley running nearly north-south at approximately 353° and a second ley running roughly east-west at approximately 83°. These lines would bear further investigation. Interestingly, a large grotto was found in the Glynne Valley and converted into pleasure gardens (with waterfalls and ponds) in 1636. King Charles I and Queen Henrietta opened them. They have not been maintained.

The Walk

The Hoar Stone

1. With your back to the Bell Inn, go right along the pavement of the A34. Turn right at a crossroads along the B4022 towards Charlbury. Pass a sports field on your right. Reach a crossroads. Turn left for 20 yards. See the hoarstone shaded by trees on your right.

2. Retrace your steps to the crossroads and go ahead, as signposted for Lidstone. Pass another side of the sports field on your right. Pass the Spinneys (a cul-de-sac) on your right. Pass the turning to Lidstone on your left. Reach the A34, go left, then turn right to cross it carefully near the bus shelter. Continue along the lane beyond the Green, passing a telephone box on your left.

3. When the lane bends left, go ahead through a kissing gate beside a fieldgate. Take the signposted public footpath to Church Enstone. Descend to a footbridge. Go ahead along a wooden causeway and over a second footbridge. Climb steps to follow the unploughed field path ahead. Cross a stile in the far corner and bear left to a stile under a tree. Follow an enclosed path. Turn left to cross a stile at the end of this path, then bear right to reach the B4030. Cross this road carefully to approach the Crown Inn.

4. Facing the Crown Inn, go right towards St. Kenelm's Church. This young King of Mercia was murdered by his ambitious sister in 822. Turn right along the lane back to the B4030. Turn left along its pavement, then take a lane on your right. Reach the B4022 and cross it carefully.

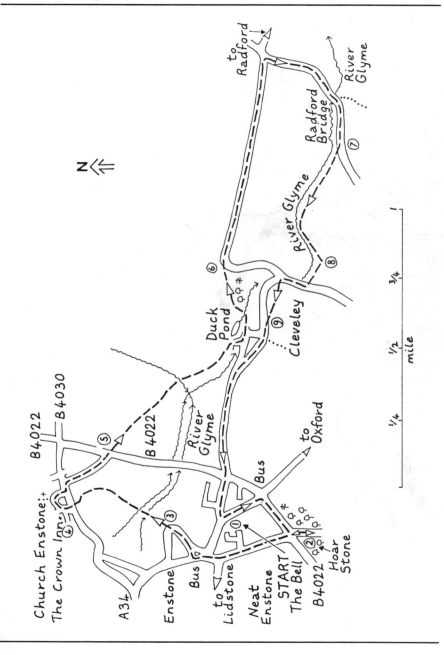

5. Go ahead along the signposted public bridleway to Cleveley. This begins with a hedge on your right. Eventually follow a section of a lane and skirt a large duck pond on your left. Reverting to a Bridleway, continue beside the River Glyme on your left. Turn left over a footbridge and follow the path past trees on your right up to a lane.

6. Go straight ahead up this lane. There is a view across to Ditchley Park on your right. This featured in Sir Walter Scott's 'Woodstock'. Sir Winston Churchill made it his weekend headquarters during Word War II. Reach a crossroads and turn right towards Enstone. Cross the narrow River Glyme at Radford Bridge. Ignore a way-marked bridleway on your left. Turn right with the lane to walk with the meandering river on your right.

7. When the lane begins to bear left, away from the river, go through a gate on your right next to a way-marked post. Go ahead along a meadow with the willow-lined river on your right. Pass under a power line and turn left through a gate in the corner. Keep the river on your right until it bears right. Go straight ahead, bearing away from the river. Follow a fence on your right for 75 yards.

8. Turn right over a stile. Cross a meadow, walking parallel to the river on your right. Go over a stile beside a gate next to a signpost in the corner ahead. Turn right down a lane. Reach a lane junction near Barnbrook House. Turn left through a gate to take a signposted bridleway over lush pasture. Cross a stile beside a signpost in the far top corner of this field.

9. Go left along the road. Pass a signposted and hedged bridleway, then a telephone box, on your left. Pass a signposted stile on your right. Go ahead to reach the B4022. Cross this road carefully and take Cleveley Road ahead into Enstone. Reach the A34 and turn left. The Bell Inn is across the road on your right.

6. *Heyford*

Route: The Bell Inn, Lower Heyford – Oxford Canal – Rousham Eyecatcher – Steeple Aston – Rousham House – The Bell Inn, Lower Heyford.

Distance: 5 miles.

Map: O.S. Pathfinder 1069 Bicester.

Start: The Bell Inn, Lower Heyford (Grid Reference SP 486248).

Access: Heyford has a station on British Rail's line between Oxford and Banbury, so come here by train. A slower method would be to steer a canal barge to Heyford's canal basin. If you must drive, Lower Heyford is on the B4030 and there is room to park cars near the pub.

The Bell Inn, Lower Heyford (0869 47176)

Tetley, Burton's and Adnam's real ale are served here. This is a very old pub in an even older building. Originally three houses, it served as a chapel becoming a pub in 1602. Meals and bar snacks are available. Opening hours are 11 am to 2.30 pm and 7 pm to 11 pm on weekdays, 12 noon to 3 pm and 7 pm to 10.30 pm on Sundays.

Heyford

Long before the railway or the canal, this was an important ford over the River Cherwell at

the time of the hay harvest. A bridge stood at Lower Heyford by 1279
and part of the 13th century structure is probably retained in the current
model, dating from the 15th century. The Americans in the nearby
airforce base must find such facts mind-boggling. Not that they have to
leave their base, with its supermarket taking dollars.

The Rousham Eyecatcher and Rousham House

William Kent was the architect and landscape gardener who designed
the Horse Guards in London in 1745. The garden at Rousham is another
memorial to his work. First, however, you encounter a strange sight on
the way to steeple Aston. A mock castle gateway with three arches
stands in the middle of a field. It terminates the view looking north from
Rousham. This mansion was built for Sir Robert Dormer in 1635. A
century later, Kent remodelled it, although most of the original interior
was left intact. The gardens are the chief attraction, with cascades and
ponds plus classical connections. They are open daily (10 am – 4.30 pm),
while the house is open on Wednesdays, Sundays and Bank Holidays
(2 pm – 4.30 pm), between April and September. Dogs and children are
not welcome (Tel. 0869 47110). The Church of St. Peter and St. Paul in
nearby Steeple Aston dates from at least the 12th century. The stump of
a 15th century cross can be seen facing the south porch, while inside the
south door are pictures and a description of a 14th century embroidered
cope which is now on permanent loan to the Victoria and Albert
Museum, London.

The Walk

1. With your back to the Bell Inn, go left and turn left immediately to
walk down Freehold Street. Bear left at a fork down Mill Lane to the
canal. Cross a bridge and turn right to follow the towpath of the canal,
on your right. Continue between the River Cherwell, on your left, and
the canal. Pass bridge 204 and Allen's Lock on your right. Soon reach a
new bridge.

2. Just before the new bridge over the canal, bear left up the grassy slope
and turn left to take a flat bridge across the River Cherwell. Bear right
with the river on your right. Cross a flat bridge over a second channel of

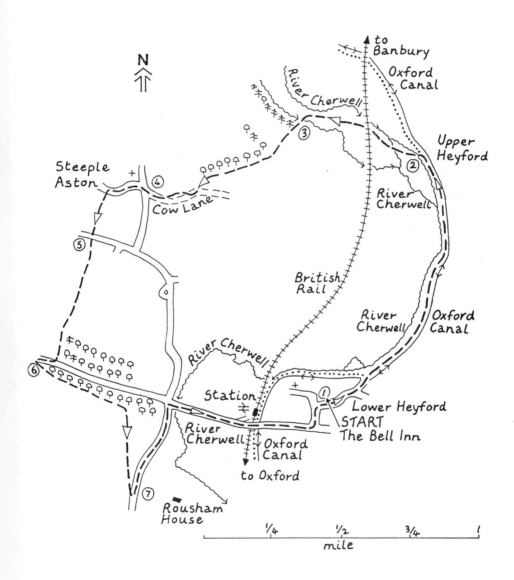

the river. Bear right to go through a tunnel under the railway just to the left of the railway bridge over the River Cherwell. Continue across a meadow, with the river on your right. Look for a wooden footbridge with a metal rail over a stream on your left.

3. Turn left across the footbridge. Follow the path up a slope to a Way-mark post (painted white at its top). Go ahead along the well-trodden path across a field, walking parallel to the hedge on your left. Take the gap in the hedge ahead, way-marked by another white-topped post. Continue through a wooden gate and bear slightly right, as directed by a yellow arrow, to follow the edge of the field. Keep a fence (and trees) on your right. Notice the three arched Rousham Eyecatcher in the field on your left. Eventually, go through a small metal gate when you come to a corner. Go right up a track for 25 yards and bear right to a way-marked stile. Cross it, follow the hedge on your right and emerge over a stile beside a small metal gate onto Cow Lane. Go ahead into Steeple Aston.

4. Bear right at a road junction to the church (dedicated to St. Peter and St. Paul). Go along North Side, passing the church on your right. Turn left down a signposted footpath which runs between two walls to a metal kissing gate. Climb with a wall on your left to a wooden kissing gate leading to a walled path to a road.

5. Cross the road to take the signposted footpath ahead, going over a stone stile. Bear left to join a track and go right along it. When the wooden fencing on your left ends, go ahead along a track which divides an open field and narrows to a footpath as it approaches the way-marked gap in a hedge ahead. Descend a rough bank to a stile beside a small, way-marked, wooden gate. Go ahead past woodland on your left. Reach a way-marked gate in the corner, beside a signpost. Cross a stile to the right of it and turn right along a road for about 100 yards.

6. When the trees on your left come to an end, cross the road carefully and turn sharply left along an old green track running above the woodland. Reach a wooden gate beside a (broken) stile in a corner. Bear right to cross the next field diagonally. Pass close to a tree-lined pond on your left. There is a view of Rousham House on your left soon afterwards.

7. Take a gate in the far corner and turn left along a road. Turn right at a crossroads (with traffic lights). Cross a bridge over the River Cherwell. There is a view of Rousham House on your right just before it is necessary to cross the road in order to continue along the pavement. A slip road on your left gives access to Heyford railway station. Go ahead over a bridge across the railway, then the canal. Continue up the road. Turn left along The Lane into Lower Heyford and the Bell Inn.

7. Woodstock

Route: The Marlborough Arms, Woodstock – Sturdy Castle Inn – Akeman Street – Oxford Canal – Rock of Gibraltar Inn – Shipton-on-Cherwell – The Marlborough Arms, Woodstock.

Distance: 10 miles.

Map: O.S. Pathfinder 1092 Woodstock.

Start: The Marlborough Arms, Woodstock (Grid Reference SP 446168).

Access: Buses stop just outside the Marlborough Arms in Woodstock. There's a good daily service between Oxford and Chipping Norton (Nos. 20, 20A, 20B and 20C) and a bus (No. X64) on Sundays and Bank Holidays only between Good Friday and the end of September which links Oxford with Swindon via Woodstock, Witney and Lechlade.

The Marlborough Arms, Woodstock (0993 811227)

This 15th century coaching inn is the Duke of Marlborough's local. It can boast two well-authenticated ghosts. One is of a young woman in Elizabethan dress at the foot of the stairs in the entrance area. The other appears about 2.30 am in room 4, where you can stay overnight. It is of a first world war army officer who gazes out of the window into the darkness. Before retiring for an interesting night, fortify yourself with a‘ meal from the restaurant or a bar snack. Real ale is available and the opening hours are 11 am to 11 pm on weekdays, 12 noon to 3 pm and 7 pm to 10.30 pm on Sundays.

Sturdy Castle Inn (086983 328)

The Oxfordshire Way follows Akeman Street (the Roman road from Cirencester to St. Alban's via Alchester) to this 'potato pub' with its potato dishes, including a vegetarian celery and cashew nut risotto served with jacket potato and salad. Real ale is available and the opening hours are 11 am to 11 pm on weekdays, 12 noon to 3 pm and 7 pm to

10.30 pm on Sundays. The inn sign depicts one man murdering another. This may refer to the origin of this pub's name. Sturdy and Castle may have been two highwaymen who fell out over how their proceeds were shared.

The Rock of Gibraltar Inn, Enslow (0869 83223)

The Oxfordshire Trek follows the towpath of the Oxford Canal to this famous pub. Built in 1787 by a contractor on the canal construction, it has many relics of its historic past, including a restored dog turn-spit above the open hearth of the bar and restaurant. It even has its own book, recording the first 200 years of the pub (by Vanadium Humphries). The name comes from the visit of General Eliott, the heroic

Governor of the Rock of Gibraltar, to Oxford in 1787. He had resisted French and Spanish attacks and was awarded the freedom of the city. He is known to have visited nearby Blenheim Palace. Children will love the canalside garden near the moorings for barges. Food and real ales are served. The opening hours are 11 am to 11 pm on weekdays, 12 noon to 3 pm and 7 pm to 10.30 pm on Sundays. The landlady's husband is a keen walker.

The Rock of Gibraltar

Disaster!

Christmas Eve, 1874, brought tragedy to the Great Western Railway's line between Hampton Gay and Shipton-on-Cherwell. The train from London to Wolverhampton was passing here at about 40 mph around noon. It was packed with people travelling home for Christmas. An extra coach had been connected at Oxford, where a second engine was also found to pull the weight (two extra coaches had been added earlier, at Reading). The train had just crossed the bridge over the River Cherwell at Hampton Gay and was approaching the old station at Shipton-on-Cherwell (where later, between 1890 and 1954, a line financed by the Duke of Marlborough was to branch off for Woodstock) when the second engine's driver noticed that the alarm bell's rope was being tugged.

For some reason it wasn't properly connected and the bell didn't ring. The brakes were quickly applied, but too late to stop the rear portion of the train from crashing down the embankment into the meadows next to the Oxford Canal. The extra carriage connected at Oxford had a broken wheel-tire. Men from nearby Hampton Gay paper mills ran to help the survivors. An Oxford surgeon happened to be in the area, while a London doctor was on the train. They could do nothing to help the 26 dead, however. Some of the carriages ended up in the Oxford Canal, beside the route of this walk (the towpath goes under the railway bridge). Snow was falling and the telegraph lines were down. It was dark before Lord Randolph Churchill (Sir Winston's father) could arrive with food and drink for the injured. More doctors came on a special train from Oxford, where 50 were taken to the Radcliffe Infirmary. Others went to vacant hotel and college bedrooms. The final death toll was 30.

The Walk

1. With your back to the Marlborough Arms, go right. Turn right along Upper Brook Hill. Pass Glyme Close on your left, then follow the road as it bends left to pass Green Lane on your right. The metalled road ceases at the sewage works, on your right.

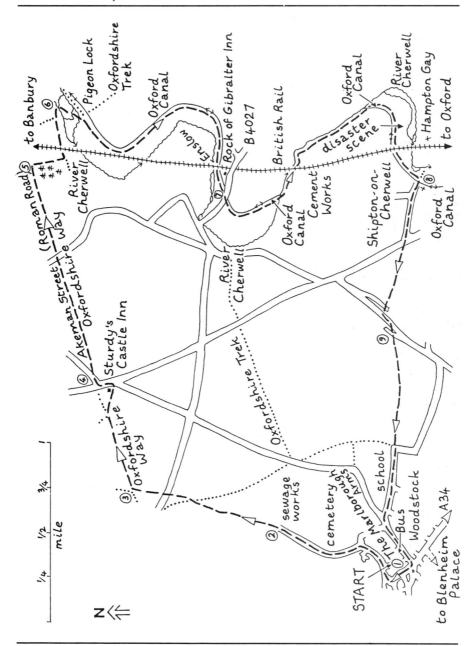

2. Go ahead along the way-marked hedged path. Emerge at the corner of a field, ignore a small, way-marked, wooden gate on your left. Go ahead with the hedge on your right. Cross a road to continue along a hedged bridleway.

3. At the crosspath with the way-marked Oxfordshire Way, turn right to follow a power line across an open field. Go ahead through a gap in a hedge and cross another field. Turn right at a junction to take a hedged path which emerges beside Sturdy's Castle Inn. Turn left to pass it before crossing the road carefully.

4. Turn right along the Tackley road for 150 yards. Bear right over a stile beside a gate to follow the signposted Oxfordshire Way. Walk beside a hedge on your left along the course of the Roman Akeman Street. Go ahead across a road and over a stile to keep with the signposted Oxfordshire Way. Eventually reach a way-mark post before a footbridge.

5. Go ahead over the footbridge and turn right across a stile. Follow the well-trodden field path towards a white cottage. Cross a stile beside a gate to take the signposted Oxfordshire Way left along a rough lane. Go under a railway bridge and pass a way-marked bridleway on your left.

6. Turn right over a flat, concrete, bridge. Take the enclosed path to Pigeon Lock on the Oxford Canal. Go under canal bridge 213 to walk along the towpath with the canal on your left. Having left the Oxfordshire Way, you are now on the Oxfordshire Trek (until Enslow). Continue under a railway bridge and notice the Rock of Gibraltar Inn on the far side of the canal.

7. Go under the bridge 216. Access to the Rock of Gibraltar Inn is on your left. Continue along the canal towpath, going under a new road bridge. Keep the canal on your left as you pass Baker's Lock and go under a railway bridge. Turn left over the bridge after Shipton Weir Lock to continue with the canal on your right. Go under another railway bridge (the scene of the 1874 disaster). Look across the meadow on your left to see the railway bridge over the River Cherwell. Pass under canal bridge 220 and turn left up to the track which crosses it.

8. Cross the bridge over the canal and follow the lane through Shipton-on-Cherwell. Keep left at a fork. Cross the main road carefully

to take a stile in the hedge opposite. Go ahead walking parallel to a hedge on your left. Bear right to follow a drainage ditch on your left to an old section of road. Cross this to the modern road and go left along its wide, grassy, verge for 250 yards.

9. Turn right across the road carefully. Cross a subsequent old section of road and go through a stile beside a gate ahead. The well-trodden field path bears slightly left to a stile in the far hedge. Continue with a hedge on your right. Take the gap in a corner ahead. Cross one more field to reach a road. Go ahead along its pavement into Woodstock, soon passing a swimming pool and a school on your right. Turn right at Oxford Street back to the Marlborough Arms.

Pigeon Lock

8. Otmoor

Route: The Red Lion Inn, Islip – Oxfordshire Way – Noke – Otmoor – Oddington – The Red Lion Inn, Islip.

Distance: 6 miles.

Map: O.S. Pathfinder 1092 Woodstock.

Start: The Red Lion Inn, Islip (Grid Reference SP 528142)

Access: A rare ray of sunshine appeared through the dark clouds besetting our railway network when Islip station was reopened in 1989. Passenger services on the line between Oxford and Bicester had resumed the year before, after a wait of 20 years. The armament depots south of Bicester had kept the line open for freight. So, do your duty (a pleasurable one) and come here by train. There is also a bus service between Oxford and Bicester via Islip, run by Charlton-on-Otmoor Services (Tel. 086733 249).

The Red Lion Inn, Islip (08675 5367)

Children will love this pub with its swings in the beer garden. There is also a skittles alley. Vegetarians are catered for in the restaurant, while snacks are available at the bar. Real ale is served in this very old pub, possibly dating from the 16th century. Opening hours are 11 am to 2.30 pm and 6 pm to 11 pm on weekdays, 12 noon to 3 pm and 7 pm to 10.30 pm on Sundays.

Otmoor

Otmoor is one of those places that planners and 'the Authorities' detest. It is a wilderness and therefore fit only to be destroyed. There is nowhere else like it in Oxfordshire. Sadly it is not what it used to be, but come after a wet period and you will see floods despite the effort made in the 19th century to drain the area.

Level and surrounded by higher land, 'Otta's fen' as its name means, is a huge swamp on top of a deep layer of clay. The Romans didn't flinch from driving their road between Alchester and Dorchester across it, but they had to construct a causeway. The inhabitants of the local villages valued this waterlogged emptiness. When flooding turned it into a shallow lake in winter, it provided them with abundant fish and wildfowl.

There was excellent rough grazing in the summer, common to all. The 'improvers' couldn't resist procuring it, however. The Duke of Marlborough sought to gain permission to drain a section of the moor in 1801. The enclosure of Otmoor was approved by Parliament in 1815. The surrounding villages were given a chance to share ownership on condition they bore their share of the costs of drainage work, plus erecting hedges and fences. As they couldn't afford such a contribution, their interest was academic. By the time the enclosure award was actually made in 1829, the deprived commoners felt they had no option but to respond with violence. The new embankments, hedges, fences, gates and bridges were destroyed. Police and troops had to be drafted in to keep the peace. When some locals were arrested in September, 1830, they escaped upon reaching Oxford in their prison cart. St. Giles' Fair was in full swing and gave them the ideal cover to confuse the authorities. Eventually, the River Ray had a new artificial channel on the northern side and a patchwork of fields developed on the loam.

When Charles Dodgson, the Oxford don better known as Lewis Carroll, looked down upon Otmoor's pattern, it inspired the chessboard in his 'Through the Looking Glass' (or so they say here – inevitably there is another claimant, being the view over the Gloucestershire plain from Leckhampton Hill, which Dodgson visited with Alice in 1863. The book was set in that year but published in 1871).

Otmoor is still a wildlife sanctuary. Teal, widgeon and pintail winter here, while water plants fill the wide ditches in the summer and lapwing, reed buntings and snipe breed here. Progress is when rare butterflies succeed where poverty-stricken commoners failed. Plans for a reservoir were dropped in the 1960s while the M40 was kept clear of here after effective campaigning in the 1980s. The one place that didn't really add its voice to the protests was Noke, but this place is notoriously reticent ('I went to Noke and nobody spoke'). It must have been an ancient sacred grove, as its name ('by the oak trees') implies.

The present church dates from the 13th century, although the font was given by Gundreda, the youngest daughter of William the Conqueror and the Lady of the Manor of Noke. Edward the Confessor was born in Islip in 1004. Its royal connection failed to prevent Cromwell routing the Royalist cavalry here on St. George's Day, 1645. Nowadays this gem of a village is visited by both the Oxfordshire Way and the Oxfordshire Trek. Robert Graves, the novelist and poet, lived in one of the cottages to your right soon after leaving Islip by the bridge over the River Ray. He lived here, where the Oxfordshire Trek bears right from the Wheatley Road, in the years after the first world war.

The Walk

1. With your back to the Red Lion Inn, go right along Islip's High Street, passing St. Nicholas' Church away to your right. Fork left down Kings Head Lane. Go ahead at the crossroads by the Swan Inn. Follow the Wheatley Road over the bridge across the River Ray. Ignore signposted paths (including the Oxfordshire Trek) on your right.

2. Notice a signpost on the right hand side of the road but pointing left. Turn left over a way-marked stile in the hedge to the left of a gate. This is the Oxfordshire Way (with OW superimposed on the yellow arrow). Go ahead 30 yards along a concrete track and bear right, just before a gate across it, to take a rough track past allotments. Continue over a stile beside a gate to follow a hedge on your right to a stile in the next corner. Maintain your direction over this and four more stiles, following the well-trodden path across four fields. Walk with a hedge on your left to a stile leading to an enclosed path.

3. Emerge at a road. Go left to follow this access road through Noke. Pass the Plough Inn and St. Giles' Church on your left.

4. The road crosses a stream and is then crossed by the signposted Oxfordshire Way (a stile on each side of the road). Go ahead along the road, as signposted 'Bridleway Oddington $1^1/_2$'.

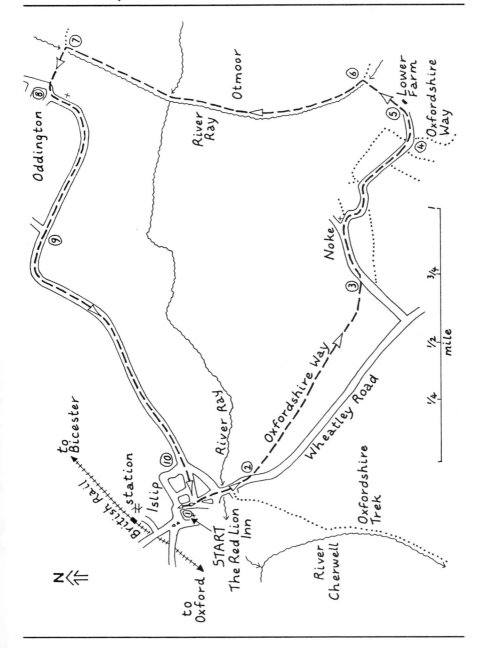

5. Just before Lower Farm, turn left along a track which is way-marked with a blue arrow. Cross the River Ray by the bridge ahead.

6.Turn left along what begins as an embankment path above the river on your left. The wilds of Otmoor are on your right. Becoming a broad track, go ahead over a flat concrete bridge across another channel of the river.

7. When the broad track ends, turn left over a flat concrete bridge. Follow another broad track into Oddington.

8. Turn left along a road. Pass St. Andrew's Church on your left. Keep to this minor road.

9. Reach a road junction and go straight ahead, as signposted, to Islip. This road is part of the Oxfordshire Cycleway.

10. Entering Islip, pass North Street on your right and Lower Street on your left. Go ahead along Middle Street, towards the tower of St. Nicholas' Church. Turn right in the High Street to return to the Red Lion Inn, on your left.

9. Asthall

Route: The White Hart Inn, Minster Lovell – The Maytime Inn, Asthall – The Swan Inn, Swinbrook – The Swan Hotel, Minster Lovell – The White Hart Inn, Minster Lovell.

Distance: 7 miles.

Map: O.S. Pathfinder 1091 Burford and Witney (North).

Start: The White Hart Inn, Minster Lovell (Grid Reference SP 315110).

Access: The White Hart Inn, Minster, stands near a bus stop served by buses Nos. V20 (Oddington – Witney, Tuesdays and Thursdays only, Tel. 0451 30403 for times), 53 (Tewkesbury – Oxford, daily, Tel. 0242 574444 for times), 64 (Swindon – Witney, weekdays only, Tel. 0242 574444 for times), Jeff's Coaches (Witney – Moreton-in-Marsh, some Tuesdays only, Tel. 0993 0779933 for times) and N. C. Wilson (Bourton-on-the-Water – Witney, Wednesdays only, Tel. 0451 21165 for times). Given this myriad of obscure and infrequent services, the least you can do is arrive by bus. Of course, you could always combine this route with No. 10 and start from Witney, which has frequent bus services from and to Oxford. Allow time to walk a total of $14^1/_2$ miles and pass yet another pub or two! Minster Lovell is on the B4047 two miles west of Witney. There is a car park for patrons at the start of this walk.

The White Hart Inn, Minster Lovell (0993 775255)

A ghost of a lady who hung herself on a now demolished spiral staircase after her suitor rejected her is vigorously authenticated by the locals. Why not try bed and breakfast here? Donnington's real ales and food will fortify you, while there is a beer garden and children are welcome. Douglas Hurd may call by for a pint, as may Jeremy Clarkson of BBC2's 'Top Gear'. Opening hours are 11 am to 11 pm on weekdays, 12 noon to 3 pm and 7 pm to 10.30 pm on Sundays.

The Maytime Inn Asthall (0993 822068)

This is a modern name for an old pub. May and Tim (hence the name) bought it in a condemned state in 1975, when the pub had been closed for two years. It has been charmingly transformed. Take bed and breakfast in room No. 1 to see or feel George the ghost. Food and real ale are available. The pub used to be called 'The Three Horseshoes' and was the childhood home of Bob Arnold, the actor who gained fame as Tom Forrest in the radio series, 'The Archers'.

The Swan Inn, Swinbrook (0993 822165)

You'll find it hard to resist the pubs along this route! The landlord's wife has seen the ghost of a lady in this 16th century pub. Real ale and food are available. The opening hours are 11.30 am to 2.30 pm and 6 pm to 11 pm on weekdays, 12 noon to 2.30 pm and 7 pm to 10.30 pm on Sundays.

The Swan Hotel, Minster Lovell (0993 774441)

Non-residents are welcome at the bar here, which serves Old Speckled Hen real ale. King Richard III stayed here three times in the Middle Ages, when this was an ale house. Try bed and breakfast in the Churchill Room to see the ghost known as the White Lady. Fine meals are provided in the restaurant, complete with French waiters. Bar opening hours are 11 am to 11 pm on weekdays, 12 noon to 3 pm and 7 pm to 10.30 pm on Sundays.

Asthall

The Romans settled here, coming along Akeman Street (the road from Cirencester to St. Alban's). St. Nicholas' Church dates from the early 12th century and has a unique early stone altar. Nearby stands the Elizabethan Manor House which was the home of Lord and Lady Redesdale and their family (the Mitfords) in the early 1920s. The six 'Mitford Sisters' later became famous. Nancy wrote novels, including 'Love in a Cold Climate' and the historical work ' The Sun King' (about Louis XIV). Pamela breeds poultry in the Cotswolds, Diana married Sir Oswald Mosley, Unity befriended Hitler, Jessica became a journalist in the U.S.A. and Deborah became the Duchess of Devonshire and chatelaine of Chatsworth House, Derbyshire. Their brother Tom was killed in action in Burma in 1945.

The Manor House, Asthall

The Walk

1. Cross the road from the White Hart Inn and turn left along the pavement of the B4047. Turn right downhill to Worsham Waterworks.

2. Opposite the entrance to Worsham Waterworks, turn left through a gate to follow the signposted bridleway to Asthall (part of the Circular Walk). Follow this headland path along the foot of the field on your left, then turn left as it climbs with a hedge on your right. Turn right in the top corner and walk beside a hedge on your left to Asthall Farm. Turn left with the track past the farmhouse on your right. Reach a road and go left along it to the Maytime pub, on your right.

3. Go right from the pub to follow the road past St. Nicholas' Church, on your right. Turn right at a T junction and follow the minor road past the Manor, on your right.

4. Turn right at a crossroads, towards Swinbrook. Cross the River Windrush to the Swan Inn, on your left.

5. Turn right over a stone stile beside a Circular Walk signpost near the road sign for Swinbrook. Take the field path ahead. Cross stiles into the next meadow and follow a wall on your left. When it bears left, go straight ahead over the meadow to a way-marked stile in the far corner.

6. Follow the meadow path with the River Windrush on your right. Continue over a stile to the left of a bridge, cross a lane and take the signposted Circular Walk footpath towards Minster Lovell, keeping the River Windrush on your right.

7. Cross the stile close to the river and level with Kitesbridge Farm, away to your left. Veer slightly left, from the river. Follow a line of poles carrying an electricity or telephone line. Cross a stile beside a gate in the corner and walk with a hedge on your left. Reach a lane and turn right down it.

8. Turn left opposite John Stone's Plastics Factory (was there ever a more incongruous spot to make safety helmets?). Follow the signposted Circular Walk bridleway towards Minster Lovell. Eventually, reach a minor road and turn right down it.

9. Go right at a road junction and pass the Swan Hotel, Minster Lovell, on your left. Go ahead across the River Windrush and turn right along the pavement. Look for steps (across the lane) and bear left up them to follow a path uphill to the White Hart Inn.

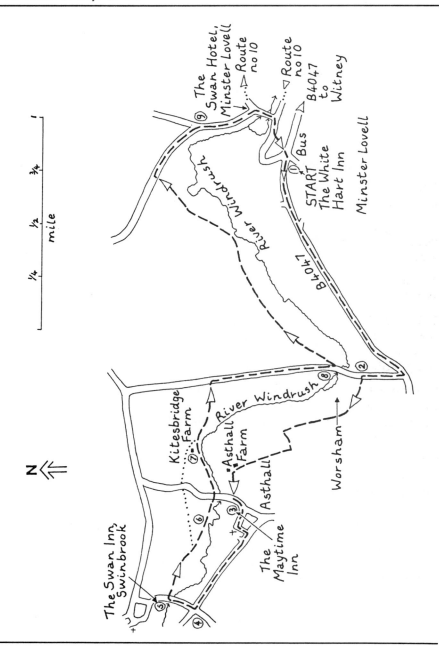

10. *Witney*

Route: The Cross Keys Inn, Witney – Pearshell Farm – The White Hart Inn, Minster Lovell – The Swan Hotel, Minster Lovell – The Cross Keys Inn, Witney.

Distance: $7^1/_2$ miles.

Maps: O.S. Pathfinder 1091 Burford and Witney (North) and 1115 Witney (South) and Carterton.

Start: The Cross Keys Inn, Witney (Grid Reference SP 356097).

Access: Witney is at the junction of the A40 and the A415. There are plenty of buses (daily) between Oxford and Carterton, but the rival companies (No.90 in red and No 100 in blue) won't accept each other's return tickets.

The Cross Keys Inn, Witney (0993 779548)

This is a very old (12th century?) inn with ghostly footsteps heard upstairs. Courage Directors is one of the real ales on offer and food is available. Opening hours are 11 am to 4 pm and 7 pm to 11 pm on weekdays, 7 pm to 10.30 pm on Sundays (not open on Sunday lunch times).

Witney

This old town is famous for its blankets. Their fame enabled the Early family's mills to survive competition from Yorkshire after the Industrial Revolution. The blankets even became popular with the Red Indians visiting the remote trading posts of the Hudson Bay Company. Also in the lovely Windrush Valley is Minster Lovell. This walk approaches the village past Charterville Allotments. Feargus O'Connor 'champion of popular rights' and MP for County Cork, bought 300 acres of land here in 1847. This was split into smallholdings and given to poor families from industrial towns. Their houses remain.

The Town Hall, Witney

Minster Lovell

As you admire the thatched cottages in the village street, note that they used to be occupied rent-free. Minster is derived from 'monasterium'. The church is dedicated to St. Kenelm, the young King of Mercia who was murdered by his ambitious sister in 822. It was dedicated to St. John until rebuilt by William, the Seventh Baron Lovell, in the 1430s. He lived in the nearby Minster Lovell Hall. Francis, the ninth Baron supported the Yorkist Richard III during the Wars of the Roses. He became powerful under the King whose crest was a wild boar. Two other royal favourites were Catesby and Ratcliffe. Hence the old piece of doggerel:

'The catte, the ratte and Lovell the dogge
Ruleth all England under the Hogge'.

Lovell's crest included a dog. He stubbornly supported the pretender Lambert Simnel when Henry VII gained the crown at Bosworth, in 1485.

The Tudor might prevailed at the Battle of Stoke, near Newark, in 1487, and Lovell had to escape capture by hiding in a secret room in his Hall. The faithful servant who fed him must have died, because he perished there. Much later, in 1708, workmen laying the foundations for a new chimney discovered the secret room with a skeleton (which quickly turned to dust) seated at a table, upon which was a book, pen and paper.

The Swan Hotel, Minster Lovell

The Walk

1. Go left from the Cross Keys Inn to pass Woolgate Shopping Centre on your left, then the bus stops and the Tourist Information Centre in Witney's Town Hall. Turn right along Corn Street. Go ahead at a roundabout, up Tower Hill. Bear left after the cemetery to follow a track signposted as part of the 'Circular Walk'. Go right when the wall on your left ends and reach Fettiplace Road near the Rowing Machine Pub.

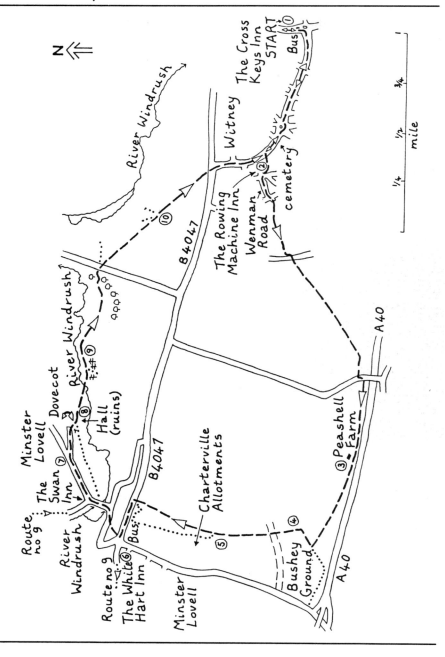

2. Go right, then left up Wenman Road. Cross an estate road and take the metalled and signposted bridleway ahead. Reach the perimeter estate road and turn left along its cyclepath for 250 yards, until a public bridleway (official diversion signpost). Turn right across the road to take the hedged path opposite. This leads to a minor road. Cross it and take the metalled track ahead to Peashell Farm. This is signposted as a bridleway and part of the Circular Walk.

3. Walk parallel to the A40 on your left and past fields on your right. When the hedge on your left ends, go ahead across a big field, as way-marked, following a power line. Reach a way-marked gap in the far hedge. Don't go through it!. Turn right (way-marked in red, for Minster Lovell) and walk with the hedge on your left for 200 yards.

4. Turn left over a stile and footbridge, way-marked as part of the Circular Walk. Bear right along an enclosed path. Cross a lane, turn left for 10 yards and turn right to resume the signposted public footpath. Walk between fences, then cross a series of way-marked stiles and emerge in a big field.

5. The right of way heads across the field to the B4047 road. A popular path seems to go beside the hedge on your left to also reach the B4047. Turn left along this road and reach the White Hart Inn, Minster Lovell.

6. Cross the B4047 from the pub and bear right across School Lane to a signposted footpath. Go down this to join the lane lower down. Cross it to the pavement and turn right to a T junction. Turn left to cross the bridge over the River Windrush. Go ahead to the Swan Hotel. Turn right along Minster Lovell's Street.

7. Fork right to St. Kenelm's Church. Pass through the ruins of Minster Lovell Hall to leave by a kissing gate. Notice a way-marked stile ahead. First, divert around to your left to see the dovecot.

8. Return to the way-marked stile, cross it and the small footbridge immediately after. Go over the meadow to a more substantial footbridge and use it to cross the River Windrush. Walk with the river on your left and through a plantation of trees. Pass a wooden gate on your right and bear left along a track between trees.

9. Emerge at the corner of a field. Go ahead beside a hedge on your right. Ignore a stile on your right but cross a stile in the far corner ahead. Continue over three more stiles to enter woodland. Follow the path to a stile in the top fence. Go ahead to a road. Go through a gate opposite, near a signpost. Bear right diagonally across a field to a stile in the far corner.

10. Go ahead to cross a stile beside a small metal gate and follow the path to reach a road at a T junction. Go ahead down Tower Hill, into Witney. Retrace your steps from the roundabout along Corn Street and go left to the Cross Keys Inn (on your right after the Woolgate Shopping Centre).

11. *Cumnor*

Route: The Vine Inn, Cumnor – Bablock Hythe – River Thames – Farmoor Reservoir – The Vine Inn, Cumnor.

Distance: 5 miles.

Map: O.S. Pathfinder 1116 Oxford.

Start: The Vine Inn, Cumnor (Grid Reference SP 463041).

Access: Cumnor is on the western edge of Oxford, just beyond the ring-road. There is a regular weekday bus service from Oxford (nos.42 and 43) plus the no. 66 bus which runs between Oxford and Swindon.

The Vine Inn, Cumnor (0865 862567)

Real ale is served in this pub, which dates from 1743. There is a beer garden and food is available. There is a car park for patrons. Opening hours are 11 am to 2.30 pm and 6 pm to 11 pm on weekdays, 12 noon to 3 pm and 7 pm to 10.30 pm on Sundays.

Tragedy and Romance

Nine parsons had to come from Oxford to lay the ghost of Amy Robsart at Cumnor. Amy was the wife of Robert Dudley, the childhood sweetheart of Queen Elizabeth I. She stood in the way of Dudley marrying the queen. Interestingly, Welsh legend affirms that the young Elizabeth did go through some ceremony of betrothal with Dudley and that she secretly gave birth to his son near Llangollen, Clwyd. The boy was brought up as Francis Bacon and was the real writer of the plays attributed to William Shakespeare.

Events changed dramatically in the mid-16th century and Elizabeth's accession to the throne in 1558 followed the uncertainties created by her sister Mary's reign, from 1553. The young Dudley had married Amy in 1550, in King Edward VI's short reign, and was imprisoned by Mary for conspiring with his father, the Duke of Northumberland, to make Lady Jane Grey queen. He soon found favour at Elizabeth's court, being appointed Master of the Horse. Amy saw little of her husband and didn't have a home of her own. She stayed at houses of friends and may have been depressed, even suicidal. Whilst staying at Cumnor Place, she died in suspicious circumstances on Sunday, 8th September, 1560. She had sent all her servants to Abingdon Fair for the day. When they returned, Amy was dead. She had ostensibly fallen down the stairs and broken her neck. A full inquiry concluded that her death was accidental. Many were prepared to believe that the ambitious Dudley had his wife strangled and thrown down the stairs. Her husband heard the news at Windsor Castle, where he didn't seem to be affected by it.

He didn't attend his wife's funeral in St. Mary's Oxford. Queen Elizabeth didn't marry him but Dudley was created Earl of Leicester within three years. Sir Walter Scott enlarged upon the story in 'Kenilworth'. Cumnor Place, which stood west of the Church, was demolished in 1810. Inside the church is a fine statue of Queen Elizabeth I, reputedly erected by Dudley. The path to Bablockhythe is an ancient route. A ferry is known to have carried wayfarers across the River Thames here since 904 to the late 20th century (sadly, it is no more). There was probably a ferry in Roman times (a Roman stone altar has been dredged up). In 1853, Matthew Arnold wrote of the 'Scholar Gipsy', who:

> '...at the ferry Oxford riders blithe,
> Returning home on summer nights, have met
> Crossing the stripling Thames at Bablockhythe,
> Trailing in the cool stream they fingers wet,
> As the punt's rope chops round.'

This is also where a beautiful barmaid (Betty Rudge from the Ferryboat Inn, now closed, across the river) fell in love with a titled undergraduate – William Flower, Viscount Ashbrook. They married in 1766 and had a son the next year. Sadly, two other children died in infancy and the Viscount died in 1780, aged 37. His widow died in 1808, aged 63.

The Vine Inn

The Walk

1. With your back to the Vine, go right along the pavement. Pass St. Michael's Church and the site of Cumnor Place on your left. Pass a bus shelter on your right (Note: most buses don't stop here!). Fork left along the Appleton Road for 100 yards.

2. Turn right along the signposted public footpath to pass a duckpond on your left, then bear right between walls. Soon turn left over a stile and follow the fence and hedge on your left to another stile in the next corner. Cross it to continue with a hedge now on your right. Turn right in the corner (away from the football pitch). Follow the path to its junction with a lane and turn left to pass a thatched cottage (No. 43) on your left and go along the lane signposted as a bridleway to the Thames and Bablockhythe.

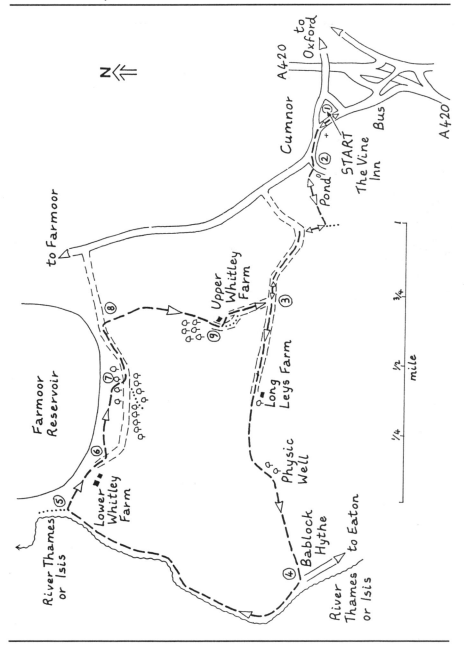

3. Keep straight ahead when the lane bears right. Take a gate ahead to follow the lane towards Long Leys Farm. Pass this farm and its orchard on your left. Proceed along a muddy track to the old ferry crossing.

4. Turn right over a stile beside a gate to walk with the river on your left. Continue through a gate, along an enclosed path and through another gate.

5. Turn right, away from the river. Follow a fence on your left up a long, narrow, meadow. Cross a stile in the far corner, pass a farmhouse (Lower Whitley Farm) on your right and take the stile ahead to continue along a lane.

6. Turn left over a footbridge to cross a stile and follow a way-marked field path beside the perimeter fence of Farmoor Reservoir on your left. This rises to give you a view of the water (and the yachts sailing on it). Descend with the fence on your left to a stile in the corner. Cross this and a subsequent footbridge to enter woodland.

7. Follow the woodland path to a gate. Reach a lane and turn left to follow it out of the wood. See the reservoir again on your left.

8. Turn right over a footbridge and stile into a field. Go ahead beside a fence on your right. Pass under power lines and bear right, as signposted. Cross a stile in the hedge ahead. Maintain this direction to a stile in the far corner, near a wood. Cross it and follow a fence on your right to a gate in the next corner.

9. Go ahead past a barn of Upper Whitley Farm on your left. Turn left to join a concrete farm access lane. Cross this and a stile opposite to follow a path across grass to a gate on your left near a tennis court. Go right, as way-marked, along a lane away from the farm. Rejoin your outward route at the fork. Turn left to retrace your steps to the pub.

12. *Godstow*

Route: The Trout Inn, Godstow – Oxford Canal – River Thames – The Trout Inn, Godstow.

Distance: 6 miles.

Map: O.S. Pathfinder 1116 Oxford.

Start: The Trout Inn, Godstow (Grid Reference SP 484093).

Access: The Trout Inn lies beside the Godstow Road near a backwater of the River Thames. This is just west of Lower Wolvercote, where the City Nippa buses from Debenham's in Oxford City Centre have their terminus in Webb's Close. Telephone 0865 778849 for details of these buses. There is a car park for patrons just across the road from the pub. If you're in a boat on the River Thames, or even a barge on the Oxford Canal, you'll find this pub very convenient. Coming to Oxford by train would deposit you near the southern end of this walk. Go down the station access road and turn right. Just before the bridge over the River Thames at Osney, turn right to follow the towpath beside the river on your left. This leads to a footbridge over the backwater which connects river and canal. Cross it to join this circuit at point 5.

The Trout Inn, Godstow (0865 54485)

This must be the most historic pub in Oxfordshire. It can also boast a delightful riverside setting and a charming atmosphere. There is even wildlife in abundance, with the pub owning the island between it and Godstow Lock. Peacocks roam, while shoals of chub grow fat in the protection of the weir stream, safe from anglers but providing a diversion for drinkers on the pub's riverside terrace.

Real Ale is served and the restaurant has an excellent reputation. Be here at midnight to see the ghost of Fair Rosamund. She can only be seen from the knees up because she has her feet on the old floor. She probably lost her virginity to King Henry II here. Unfortunately, the King was married at the time and the pub was a high-class brothel.

Beautiful girls were available from nearby Godstow Nunnery, where Rosamund had been sent by her father, Walter de Clifford, to finish her education. Henry's royal palace of Woodstock was conveniently close by. The king took Fair Roz there and set her up as his mistress. Tradition states that his queen, Eleanor of Aquitaine, was not amused. She poisoned her rival, whose body was buried at Godstow.

The Trout

Royal endowments paid for silken curtains around the tomb and continuous prayers for Rosamund's soul. Bishop Hugh of Lincoln didn't approve of all this in 1191 and ordered the remains to be cast out. Upon his departure, the nuns gathered the bones in a bag, however, to be kept in a lead coffin in the Chapter House. When the coffin was opened at the Dissolution, it was found to smell sweetly. Rosamund bore Henry two sons, William Longspee (Earl of Salisbury) and Geoffrey (who became Lord Chancellor of England). In fact, the highly unpopular Queen Eleanor probably didn't poison Henry's paramour (or find her way through the mythical maze in order to do so). Rosamund seems to have chosen to retire to Godstow Nunnery, where she probably died of natural causes in 1176. Pilgrims flocked to her shrine. She had been confident of salvation and predicted that a tree would turn to stone when it occurred. A tree duly obliged at her death. Clearly, she was a 'Rose of the World'. Opening hours are 11am to 3pm and 6pm to 11pm on weekdays, 12 noon to 3 pm and 7pm to 10.30pm on Sundays.

The Oxford Canal

The Cherwell Valley provided the route for a canal linking Oxford and the River Thames with the industrial Midlands. Begun in 1769, it was completed in 1790 (a result of cash flow problems). Now it is popular with leisure craft (and with residents of barges). It acts as a corridor for wildlife. Linnet, goldfinch, greenfinch and bullfinch may all be seen here. Water voles feed on the vegetation. The flowery meadows between the canal and the railway which came to usurp its function in 1850 (this is the mainline between Oxford and Birmingham via Banbury) has ox-eye daisies, meadow buttercup, marsh arrow grass, lady's bedstraw, knapweed and yellow rattle. Policeman's helmet, with its explosive seed pods, likes the canal, as do meadowsweet, greater willowherb and yellow flag. Damselflies can be seen in May and June, with dragonflies in the summer.

Oxford Ragwort was brought to England from Italy for the University's Botanical Garden. It escaped and spread around the country along the railway lines. It is best seen here near the River Thames, however, at the remains of Godstow Abbey. Garrisoned for King Charles I when a private house in 1646, it was largely destroyed by the Parliamentarian forces of Colonel Fairfax. This is where Rosamund was buried, near Godstow Lock.

The Walk

1. With your back to the Trout Inn, go right along the road, which has an elevated pavement. Cross a bridge over a channel of the River Thames. Pass Webbs Close (the bus terminal) on your left. Follow Godstow Road past the White Hart Inn on your left. Take the footbridge, to the right of the road bridge, to go ahead across the railway and the canal.

2. Turn right up a road named Wolvercote Green. Pass Dove House Close on your left then, as the road turns left at the Plough Inn, bear right. Take the rough track to a bridge over the canal.

3. Cross the bridge over the canal and turn right to reach the towpath. Turn right again to go under the bridge (no 236) and walk beside the

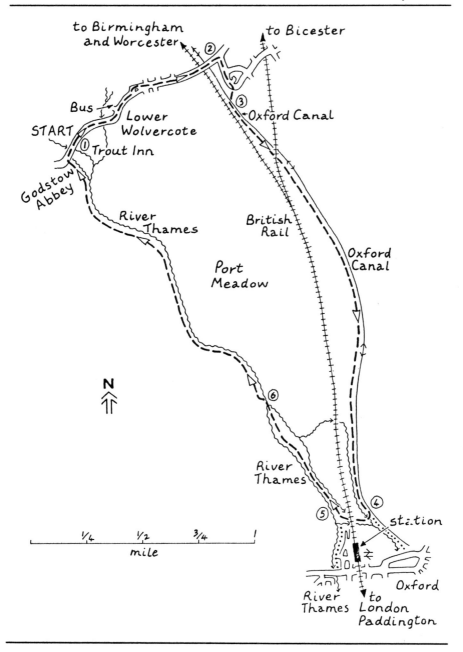

canal on your left.

4. When you are near the end of the canal in central Oxford, come to a fork. Do not bear left over bridge no 243, but do bear right over a flatter bridge. Follow the path under the railway bridge.

5. Reach the River Thames and turn right to follow its towpath. Walk with the river on your left until you pass Bossoms Boatyard. Turn left over Rainbow Bridge.

6. Continue along the towpath beside the River Thames, which is now on your right. Port Meadow is on the far side of the river. Just beyond Godstow Lock, pass the remains of Godstow Abbey, on your left. Turn right on the Godstow Road to take the bridge over the River Thames and reach the Trout Inn, on your right.

13. *Garsington*

Route: The Plough Inn, Garsington – Malthouse – Garsington House – Denton House – Southend – St Mary's Church, Garsington – Garsington Manor House – The Plough Inn, Garsington.

Distance: 4 miles

Map: O.S. Pathfinder 1116 Oxford

Start: The Plough Inn, Garsington (Grid Reference SP 580022)

Access: The Plough Inn is in the centre of the village of Garsington, by the bus shelter. Although five miles south-east of the centre of Oxford, it is only two miles from the outlying estate of Blackbird Leys. There is a good bus service on weekdays (No 201 Oxford – Watlington, Tel. 0865 711312 for latest timetable information). There is a car park at the Plough Inn.

The Plough Inn, Garsington (086736 395)

A beer house attached to a market garden has long functioned on this site. The building dates from about 1700, and it belonged to a baker in 1823 (bakers often diversified into brewing). A Roman sword found at the bottom of its garden is now in the Ashmolean Museum, Oxford. Sir John Wheeler-Bennett, who lived in the Manor House until his death in 1975, used to sup here. A distinguished historian, he was a biographer of King George VI. Courage Best and Directors Real Ale is served, while food is available. The opening hours are 11am to 11pm on weekdays, 12 noon to 3pm and 7pm to 10.30pm on Sundays.

Garsington

The agricultural labourers have gone, but this is still a tranquil spot with fine rural views. The car factories of Cowley and the estate of Blackbird Leys seem to be in another world, well away from this ancient, holy, 'Gaerse dun' (grassy hill).

The church sits on the highest ridge between Oxford and the Chilterns. This doesn't quite reach 400 feet, but it gives splendid views over the Downs, the Thames Valley, Wittenham Clumps (see the Dorchester walk) and the Chilterns. It was close enough to Oxford to boast orchards and market gardens whose produce was taken fresh into the city by horse and cart.

Most of the land is owned by colleges of Oxford University. It was held by the Roundheads during the siege of Oxford, when the city was Charles I's capital in 1645 and 1646. They stabled their horses in the church, while the Manor House witnessed Cromwell and Fairfax discussing tactics.

Famous people have always found their way to this village. Patrick Gordon-Walker, Foreign Secretary in the 1964 Labour Government, lived in Pettiwell House, near the start of this walk, before World War II.

Garsington House has a high peaked roof, which indicates that it used to be thatched. Dating from at least 1612, it belonged to Exeter College, Oxford.

The Norman tower of St Mary's Church dates from 1160. On the wall, near the font, is a memorial by Eric Gill to Lady Ottoline Morrell, who died in 1938. She was the sister of the Duke of Portland and married Philip Morrell, the M.P. for South Oxfordshire. They made Garsington Manor a sanctuary for conscientious objectors to World War I. Artists and intellectuals flocked here, including Aldous Huxley, Bertrand Russell, Virginia Woolf, D. H. Lawrence, Maynard Keynes and Siegfried Sassoon. More recently, the historian Sir John Wheeler-Bennett made it his home. He witnessed the rise of Hitler's Germany at firsthand, living in the country at the crucial time, and travelled across Soviet Russia. Thomas Chaucer, the son of Geoffrey, owned the property in the 15th century. The present house is largely a product of the 17th century.

The pond, or Gizzel, used to provide the village with water. Fed by a spring, it has recently been cleaned up by the local Scouts. Gizzel may be derived from an Old English word 'gysel', which means 'gushing'.

The Well House, on your right after passing the church on your way back to the centre of the village, stands on the site of the old rectory.

Rider Haggard, the author, lived here as a youth and befriended a local farmer called William Quartermain. He used the surname for his hero Allan Quartermain.

Opposite, in the grounds of Manor Farm House, on your left, is an old dovecote. This dates from 1762. Sir Karl Parker, Director of Oxford's Ashmolean Museum, lived in the former farmhouse between 1940 and 1962.

The Walk

1. With your back to the Plough Inn, go right, down Pettiwell. Reach a public footpath signpost on your right, opposite Lanesra Cottage. Turn right to pass Malthouse on your left and cross the stile ahead.

2. Walk beside a hedge on your right. Continue over a stile in the next corner. Cross a field, going down to a stile in the opposite fence. Go ahead along the well-trodden path in the next field to go through a way-marked gap in the hedge facing you. Bear right to reach a jutting corner. Follow the hedge on your left to a stile beside a gate. This gives access to a road (Clinkards Hill). Cross it carefully and go left, along the pavement.

3. Reach Garsington House on your right. The elevated and railed pavement divides here. Keep to the level pavement, bearing right and soon turning right through a small, way-marked gate. Walk with a wall on your right. Go ahead over a way-marked stile. Continue to a way-marked stile in the hedge facing you. Cross the next field to a stile which leads to a path between gardens to a road.

4. Turn right for 50 yards, then turn left to follow a rough lane between houses. Go ahead over a stile to follow a field path. Go down to another stile, cross it and walk with a hedge on your right for 150 yards. Turn right over a stile and turn left immediately. Walk with the hedge on your left now.

5. Go ahead over a stile and bear right to cross another stile and a footbridge. Follow the way-marks to reach a stile in the far corner. Cross it and go left to a lane.

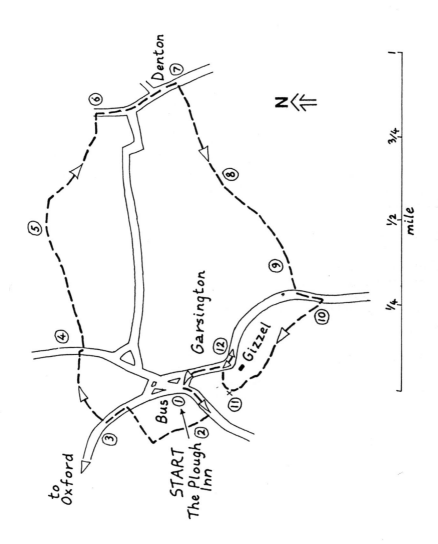

6. Go right along the lane. Pass Denton House and maintain your direction at two T junctions (ignoring a turning to the right, then one to the left).

7. Take a gate on your right to cross a farmyard. Go ahead along a track, continue down the next field to a stile, which you cross.

8. Go over a field to the gap near its corner. Bear right to the corner of a hedge and walk with it on your right. Continue over a ditch and a stone stile.

9. Take a private road but public footpath past a house and garden on your left. Reach a public road and go left along the pavement for 150 yards. This is Southend and No 93, a timber-framed house, on your left, has an owl-hole high up in the left-hand gable. Owls were encouraged in order to keep down vermin.

10. Turn right over a stile beside a gate and near a letterbox. Bear right to reach a stile in the far corner. Continue with a fence on your right. Cross a stile in the next corner and take a narrow path to a field. Go ahead to St Mary's church.

11. Pass the church on your left to leave by its lych gate. Go right down the road. Notice the Gizzel (a pond) on your right, where a signpost points out another public footpath. Go ahead along the road, however, to see the manor house on your right.

12. Turn round to walk past the church on your left, notice a dovecote on your left and turn left to return to the Plough Inn.

14. Thame

Route: The Black Horse Hotel, Thame – Thame Park – Manor Farm – Sydenham Grange Farm – The Black Horse Hotel, Thame

Distance: 7 miles

Map: O.S. Pathfinder 1117 Thame

Start: The Black Horse Hotel, Thame (Grid Reference SP 707058)

Access: The Black Horse Hotel is near the centre of Thames, on the corner of Cornmarket and Rooks Lane. Parking space is signed nearby, while buses stop near the Town Hall, at the other end of Cornmarket. Thames is served by bus No 280 (Oxford – Aylesbury) and Nos 232, 331 and 332 from High Wycombe.

The Black Horse Hotel, Thame (0844 262886)

The bar of this hotel is open on market days (Tuesdays and Saturdays) from 11am to 11pm. Otherwise, it is open from 11am to 2.30pm and 6pm to 11pm on weekdays, 12 noon to 3pm and 7pm to 10.30pm on Sundays. Bed and breakfast accommodation plus meals in the restaurant are available. This old pub is fascinating because of its name. It could well mark a watering-hole used by the sixth century knights of King Arthur,

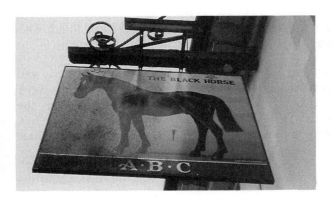

whose border with the Saxons must have been quite complicated around here, between the Saxon Thames and the Celtic Chilterns. Read all about this proposition in 'The Black Horsemen' by S. G. Wildman (John Baker, London, 1971).

Thame

Thame is named after its river, which joins the Isis near Dorchester (see route 18). The Saxons settled here and, in the 12th century, the Cistercians built an abbey to the south of the town. This was the third richest Cistercian abbey in England at the Dissolution. Its last abbot, Robert King, was compensated by being made first Bishop of Oxford. The abbey was acquired by Lord Williams of Thame. He founded the Grammar School in 1559 and its pupils were to include Milton and John Hampden. The agricultural town was put on the railway map in 1864 when the Great Western Railway built a line through it to connect Oxford with Princes Risborough (and the line from London Marylebone to Birmingham via Banbury). The rails can still be seen if you look over the bridge as this walk leaves Thame.

Passenger services on this line ceased in 1963 and the track from Princes Risborough stops here now and is for freight only – and there's not much of that by the look of the weeds. Thame has grown into a commuter town, however, needing a rail link with London. British Rail's answer has been to open a new station at Haddenham, two miles east on the London Marylebone – Banbury Chiltern Line, and call it Thame Parkway.

The Walk

1. Turn right along Cornmarket. Go ahead up Park Street. Pass the Four Horse Shoes on your left and fork right along Thame Park Road. This soon crosses the railway line.

2. Pass the gates of Thame Park on your left. Go ahead 150 yards and turn left through a way-marked gap in the hedge and over a stile. Keep to the right of way marked by white painted posts and cross the parkland to an access drive to the House (and abbey ruins) on your left. Go ahead to reach a way-marked stile in the far fence. Cross a footbridge after it.

3. Aim for the far left corner of the next field, as way-marked. Continue over another footbridge and bear slightly right towards a white

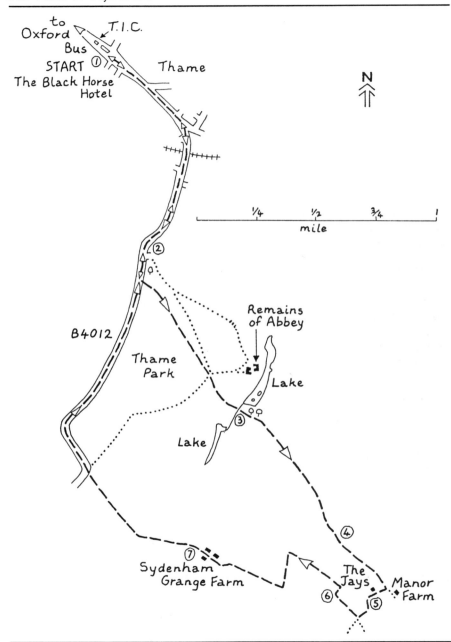

way-mark post in the next field. Go through a gateway on your left in the far corner. Follow a hedge on your right to a way-marked gate in the corner of the next field.

4. Walk along the grass and mud track with a hedge on your right. Take the metal fieldgate ahead to cross a field to Manor Farm. Go over a stile beside a gate, then turn right through a wooden gate to follow a concrete access lane (to The Jays). When this bears right to a garage, go ahead past the house along a muddy, hedged, track.

5. Take a small wooden gate way-marked with a blue arrow. Bear left. Reach a stile in the fence on your left, near a corner of a field. Don't cross it! Ignore, also, the grass track ahead. Turn right instead and walk up the field with a hedge on your left. Go ahead through a small wooden gate in the top corner.

6. Turn right to follow the headland path beside a hedge on your right. Turn left in the corner, as way-marked. Follow the hedge on your right. Continue through a small gate beside double fieldgates. Turn left with the track in the next corner and keep the hedge on your right. Turn right to Sydenham Grange Farm.

7. Go ahead along the farm access lane to the B4012 road. Bear right along this road back to Thame.

15. *Coleshill*

Route: The Radnor Arms, Coleshill – Coxwell Wood – Great Barn, Great Coxwell – The Radnor Arms, Coleshill.

Distance: 6 miles.

Map: O.S. Pathfinder 1135 Faringdon.

Start: The Radnor Arms, Coleshill (Grid Reference SU 237938).

Access: Coleshill is on the B4019 between Faringdon and Highworth. It is served by bus No. 67 between Faringdon and Swindon on Fridays only. On other weekdays, bus to Faringdon (see No. 16) and combine this route with No. 16 at the slightly staggered crossroads in Great Coxwell. Allow plenty of time for what would become a 12 mile walk.

The Radnor Arms, Coleshill (0793 762366)

Real ale is served straight from the cask at this former village smithy. It was turned into a pub in 1949 but retains old implements as mementos. Food is available, while there is a car park for patrons. Opening hours are 11 am to 2.30 pm and 6.30 pm to 11 pm on weekdays, 12 noon to 3 pm and 7 pm to 10.30 pm on Sundays.

Coleshill

Local tradition insists on a connection with Old King Cole, both here and at Cole's Pits on the other side of Faringdon. The village overlooks the River Cole, which forms the county boundary with Wiltshire. Until a major fire destroyed it in 1952, Coleshill could boast that its great house was one of the masterpieces of English architecture. Inigo Jones worked on it at the same time as the construction of Wilton House. Alfred Williams, the 'Hammerman Poet' of Swindon's Great Western Railway works, wrote about a riddle told at a fete in Coleshill in 1830:

'When first the marriage knot was tied between my wife and me, My age exceeded hers as much as three times three does three. But when ten years and a half ten years we man and wife had been her age approached as near to mine as eight is to sixteen.' Perhaps the answer should be printed upside down at the bottom of the page! When they married, the bridegroom was 45 and the bride 15. When the husband was 60, his wife was 30.

The Great Barn, Great Coxwell

Great Coxwell

This is an area which has been settled since ancient times. The hillfort (now crowned with trees) on Badbury Hill is at least 2500 years old. Its name may suggest it as a possible site for King Arthur's famous victory over the Saxons at Mount Badon, but there are sound strategical reasons to locate this at Baydon in Wiltshire. No one can doubt the size of the harvest in the 13th century, however. It was stored in the finest surviving barn in the country. Now in the care of the National Trust (open daily at any reasonable time, with somebody there to collect a fee at times), it was built by Cistercian monks in the early 13th century. It has massive stone walls, a stone-tiled roof and an interesting timber construction.

The Walk

1. With your back to the Radnor Arms, turn left and left again immediately. Reach a road junction and bear right to a signposted footpath.

2. Follow the path up the side of the field, beside a hedge on your left. Continue over a way-marked stile in the corner. Pass a patch of woodland on your right and proceed over a footbridge in the next corner. Emerge over a stile into the corner of a field. Go ahead beside a hedge on your left. Go over a stile and along an enclosed path (with a hedge on your left and a fence on your right). Cross a footbridge ahead and follow the hedge on your left around the edge of the next field.

3. Turn left over a footbridge and a way-marked stile in the hedge. Bear right diagonally across the next field to Brimstone Farm. Go over a stile in the corner and turn right to pass the farmyard on your left. Cross a concrete lane and go through the way-marked gate ahead. Walk with a wooden fence on your left.

4. Continue through a gate in the corner to reach the next field. Go ahead to join a hedge on your left. Enter Coxwell Wood and go ahead uphill along the main path, ignoring all side paths. Continue past a secluded house on your left, then walk with the rampart of Badbury Hillfort on your left. Cross the stile beside a gate ahead to reach the National Trust car park.

5. Turn left along the road for 300 yards. Turn right over a stile to follow the signposted path to Great Coxwell. When you pass woodland on your left, look for a stile and bear left over it. Follow a woodland path to emerge across a footbridge and a stile. Turn left to follow the fence on your left to the Great Barn. Cross a stile on your left to visit it and reach a road. Turn right along the road to the staggered crossroads in Great Coxwell. Here you may link with route No. 16.

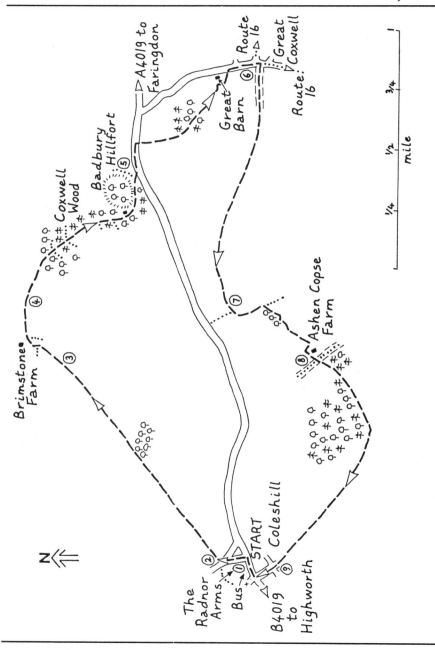

6. Turn right down Puddleduck Lane. This soon deteriorates to a rough, hedged, track. Continue through a gate along a track across pasture. Go ahead through a way-marked gate and walk parallel to the hedge on your right in the next field.

7. Take the gate in the corner and turn left along a hedged track. Pass a house on your left and turn right through a field gate to walk beside a fence on your right to a stile in the far corner. Go ahead over this and a subsequent stile to continue beside the fence on your right in the next field. Turn right over a way-marked stile and go left along a track which passes farm buildings on your left.

8. Cross a lane to take the way-marked stile beside a gate ahead. Follow a track across a beanfield and past woodland on your left, and then on your right. Bear right, as way-marked, at the end of the woodland. Cross a field towards an isolated group of trees. Maintain this direction to a stile. Go ahead over two more stiles and over fields towards Coleshill.

9. Go through a gate to enter Coleshill. Take the road ahead towards the church. Turn right along the pavement of the B4019. Pass the No. 67 bus stop to reach the Radnor Arms, on your left.

The Radnor Arms

16. *Faringdon*

Route: The Bell Hotel, Faringdon – The Folly – The Eagle Tavern, Little Coxwell – Great Coxwell – The Bell Hotel, Faringdon.

Distance: 6 miles.

Map: O.S. Pathfinder 1135 Faringdon.

Start: The Bell Hotel, Faringdon (Grid Reference SU 289955).

Access: The Bell Hotel is in the centre of Faringdon, near the bus stop and car parking space. Faringdon is at the junction of the A420 and the A417. Buses run here on weekdays from Oxford and Swindon (No. 66). Should you combine this with route No. 15 at Great Coxwell and miss the last No. 66 bus back to Oxford (there is a better service to Swindon), take comfort in an evening No. 42 bus from Faringdon to Oxford on Fridays and Saturdays only. Unfortunately, the branch line to the Great Western mainline closed in 1963, so you can no longer come here by train.

The Bell Hotel, Faringdon (0367 240534)

Cromwell's soldiers celebrated their long fight to capture Faringdon in this pub. It is said they rioted and killed one of their officers. The building dates from about 1600, but there was a watering-hole here in Saxon times. Tanglefoot is just one of the real ales on offer now, while food is available. You can stay here for bed and breakfast. Opening hours are 11 am to 11 pm on weekdays, 12 noon to 3pm and 7 pm to 10.30 pm on Sundays.

The Eagle Tavern, Little Coxwell (0367 240120)

Mark Lawrenson, of Liverpool F.C. fame, is the landlord here. A famous red shirt adorns a wall, along with action pictures of the glory days. Built around 1900, this pub serves food and is open from 12 noon to 3 pm and 7 pm to 11 pm daily (10.30 pm on Sundays).

Faringdon

Faringdon has come down in the world since its strategic position between the Downs and the Thames attracted the Saxons. Its name means 'fern-covered hill'. King Alfred had a royal manor here and his son Edward the Elder died in Faringdon in 924. Since then, it has been rudely awakened from its slumbers by two civil wars and a folly. A castle existed for a time on Folly Hill, but King Stephen (who fought Queen Matilda) demolished it in 1144. The spire of the church was destroyed in 1645, when Roundheads besieged Royalists here. Actually, it was a Parliamentarian son shooting at his Cavalier father in the manor house. The Pye family conducts its quarrels in style!

The present Faringdon House was built for his descendant, Henry Pye, who was King George III's Poet Laureate. His poems helped to drive the King mad and lose us the American colonies. He planted the trees on Folly Hill and wrote a poem (too turgid to reproduce) about the view from it, entitled 'Faringdon Hill'. Curiously, the hill acquired its name before its actual folly. This is a brick tower 140 feet high. It was erected in 1935 by Lord Berners to give work to the local unemployed. It is open on the first Sunday of each month between April and October, from 2 pm to 5 pm. Locals complained vigorously against it, with one old soldier's reference to 'Lord Berners' monstrous erection' perhaps an allusion to the lord's notoriously unmarried condition. Real men, like on old admiral, railed against him and objected to it receiving planning permission. When it was finally opened on 5th November, 1935, hundreds of doves dyed red, white and blue were released. Lord Berners left a note reading 'Members of the public committing suicide from this tower do so at their own risk'.

The Walk

1. With your back to the Bell, go right, up London Street. Turn right along the raised pavement of Stanford Road.

2. Turn left along the signed and metalled path to Folly Hill. Continue past the tower on your left to emerge from the ring of trees. Go down the field path ahead. Walk past a hedge formed by lilac bushes on your left. Go over a stile in the bottom corner.

3. Turn right to walk with the hedge on your right. Go ahead over a stile and follow the path to the road on your left. Go right to a T junction and turn left to cross the A420 carefully. Go ahead along the verge of the A417 towards Wantage for 300 yards.

4. Turn right along the signposted bridleway (part of the Circular Walk). Follow the track with a fence on your left to a signpost at an open field. Do not take the field path straight ahead, but do turn half right to follow a path diagonally across the field.

5. Join the broad track which has swung to the middle of the field from its perimeter on your right. Follow the track over a railway bridge (this branch line existed between 1878 and 1963). Pass a farm on your left, ignore its access lane on your right and take the bridleway (signposted as part of the Circular Walk) ahead.

6. Leave the Circular Walk at a signposted crosstracks by taking the bridleway ahead. Turn left at a road for 300 yards, then turn right to Little Coxwell. Reach Mark Lawrenson's Eagle Tavern.

7. Facing the Eagle Tavern, take the road ahead on your left. Bear right with this road (which has a pavement). Go ahead across the A420 with care. Turn right 50 yards, then turn left along a signposted and metalled footpath (part of the Circular Walk again) to Great Coxwell. Turn right along the village street. Pass The Laurels on your right. Reach a slightly staggered crossroads. Here you may link with the Route No. 15 to make a longer walk.

8. Turn right to pass houses called 'Old Walls' and 'Moonrakers' on your left. Turn left up a rough track as the road bends right. This is Gipsy

Lane and it may be muddy. Ignore a track to a farm on your right. Follow the muddy lane as it bends left to the B4019 road.

9. Turn right along the grass verge of the B4019 into Faringdon. Turn left at the T junction to reach the town centre and the Bell.

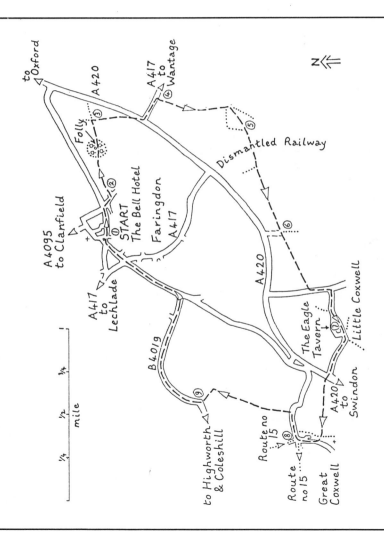

17. Abingdon

Route: The King's Head and Bell Inn, Abingdon – River Thames – The Culham Laboratory – Schola Europaea – Culham Cut – River Thames – The King's Head and Bell Inn, Abingdon.

Distance: $6^1/_2$ miles.

Map: O.S. Pathfinder 1136 Abingdon.

Start: The King's Head and Bell Inn, Abingdon (Grid Reference SU 498969).

Access: There are plenty of buses to Abingdon from Oxford, including Nos 30, X30, 31 (continues to Wantage) and 390 (continues to London). Why not come here by riverboat? Telephone Salter Bros Ltd. on 0865 243421 for details. The King's Head and Bell Inn is located near the County Hall and Museum in East St. Helen's Street.

The King's Head and Bell Inn, Abingdon (0235 520157)

Handel started to write his 'Water Music' here. The King in question is Charles I, who also gained inspiration here. Unfortunately his Council of War led to his losing the Head which is now firmly attached to the pub's old name (there is a record of a Bell Inn in 1554). See what the real ale and food can do for you in this place. Opening hours are 11 am to 3 pm and 6 pm to 11 pm on weekdays, 12 noon to 3 pm and 7 pm to 10.30 pm on Sundays.

An Old County Town

Not only has Oxfordshire taken part of Berkshire, but Abingdon was once the capital of the Royal County. Culham has always been in Oxfordshire, however. Our Neolithic ancestors settled in this area but they wouldn't recognise the river, which has had its course changed artificially.

The Old County Hall

Abingdon grew outside the gates of its abbey, which was the sixth richest in England at the time of the Dissolution. Most date its foundation back to the Saxons in 675. There is a legend of a Celtic hermit called Aben who was a survivor of a slaughter of the local population by Saxons led by Hengist in the fifth century, however. There is no doubt that St. Edmund of Abingdon was born here in 1170. He was canonised in 1246 after being Henry II's Archbishop of Canterbury and Roger Bacon's lecturer at Oxford University. By the 14th century, the Abbey's reputation was such that William Langland wrote in 'Piers Plowman':

'Ac there shall come a kyng and confess your religiouses,
And beat you as the Bible telleth for brekynge of your rule.
And then shal the Abbot of Abyngdone, and al his issue forever
Have a knock of a kyng, and incurable the wounde'.

The Abbey Stream is the chief memorial to the monks. The river used to follow the Back Water or Swift Ditch before the monks harnessed its water to power their mill. Later its original course was reopened, complete with an early 17th century pound lock. The present course was returned to in 1790 to bring trade back to the town. A fine 13th century exchequer building still stands (go down Checker Walk). This can be visited on any day except Good Friday and on winter Mondays, between 2 pm and 6 pm. The 12th century St. Nicholas' Church has also survived, as it was built for the abbey's lay servants. Opposite it is the old County Hall, which betrays Wren's influence on its architecture and houses a museum (open Tuesdays-Sundays, 1 pm to 5 pm April-October, 1 pm to 4 pm November-March) with a collection of buns thrown from its roof to celebrate important royal occasions. Admission is free.

The old stocks at the King's Head and Bell Inn

The Walk

1. Go right to the old County Hall and ahead to St. Nicholas' Church. Go through the gateway into the old Abbey Grounds and pass the new Tourist Information Centre on your left and Checker Walk on your right. Follow Abbey Close through a car park.

2. Turn right over a bridge across Abbey Stream and go ahead to the River Thames. Turn left to walk beside the (modern course of the) river on your right. Don't take a wooden footbridge ahead (across Abbey Stream) but do turn right across the weir and Abingdon Lock.

3. Go left to walk with the River Thames on your left. Follow the towpath and divert inland with it to cross two footbridges over two channels of the Back Water, or original Swift Ditch. Approach Nuneham Railway Bridge.

4. Turn right in the corner of the field just before the railway bridge. Walk parallel to the railway (the main line between Oxford and London Paddington via Didcot) on your left. Ignore the stile for a right of way which crosses the railway. Go ahead along the narrow, enclosed path (between the railway on your left and a private farm track on your right). Join a track coming over the bridge from the Culham Laboratory (home of the Joint European Torus, a European Community project to experiment in producing electricity by nuclear fusion).

5. Turn right, away from the railway, along the track which becomes Thame Lane. Pass Schola Europaea (this European School is housed in the former Culham teacher training college). It is notorious for allowing its pupils to smoke. Passing on a sunny summer afternoon, I noticed nobody was outside playing cricket, either. I wonder what the food is like.

6. Reach the A415 and turn right along its pavement. Pass the Waggon and Horses Inn on your left and turn left along the road to Culham.

7. Approaching a bridge over the river, turn right through a gate beside a signpost. Follow the towpath past Culham Lock. Walk with the river (actually Culham Cut, dug in 1809 to improve navigation) on your left. Ignore a footbridge across it. Reach the real River Thames and turn right

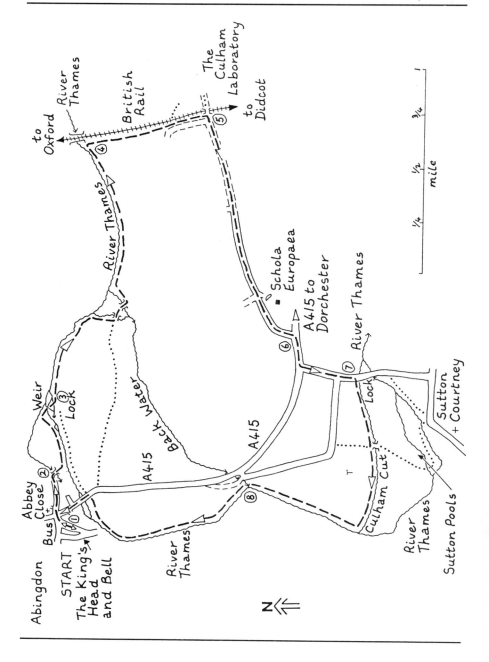

to walk with it on your left, still going upstream.

8. Cross a stile in the left hand corner of the field and go ahead over a subsequent footbridge and stile. Continue beside the Thames on your left all the way back to Abingdon Bridge. Turn left across this back to the old County Hall. Go left to retrace your steps along East St. Helen's Street to the pub where King Charles I said farewell to his Queen Henrietta Maria for the last time before he sent her to safety in France.

18. Dorchester

Route: The Fleur De Lys Inn, Dorchester – Day's Lock – Wittenham Clumps – Shillingford – The Fleur De Lys Inn, Dorchester.

Distance: 7 miles.

Map: O.S. Pathfinder 1136 Abingdon.

Start: The Fleur De Lys Inn, Dorchester (Grid Reference SU 578942).

Access: There is a good bus service to Dorchester. The No. 5 bus between Oxford and Reading runs on weekdays, while the No. 390 bus between Oxford and London runs daily. Cars can be parked near the inn.

The Fleur De Lys Inn, Dorchester (0865 340502)

This inn dates from the early 16th century. You can stay overnight here. Take the double bedroom and share it with the ghost of a girl in a headscarf and a shawl. The food is highly recommended, while real ale is served. The opening hours are 11 am to 3 pm and 6.30 pm to 11 pm from Monday to Fridays, 11 am to 11 pm on Saturdays and 12 noon to 3 pm and 7 pm to 10.30 pm on Sundays.

The Start of the River Thames

This is one of the most sacred spots in England. Instead of becoming a village, Dorchester could have developed into the capital of England. Fortunately for the tranquil, unspoilt countryside, history took a different course. The Romans had an important town here on their road between Alchester and Silchester, near where it crossed the River Thames. The Ancient Britons had made it an important market. It is the sacred nature of this bend in the river that prevails, however. An important Neolithic sacred complex is now lost where flooded gravel pits line the road north of Dorchester. It comprised a cursus and big rings. Radio-carbon analysis has dated these to 3000 BC. Whatever they were, these lost monuments were of immense importance. Castle Hill on Wittenham Clumps, with its folk memory of buried treasure guarded by a phantom raven in the eastern ditch (known as the 'Money Pit') was occupied by the Iron Age.

Most of the population had moved to the other side of the river, defended by the massive Dyke Hills, by the time of the Roman invasion. The Roman town survived until well after the withdrawal of the legions in 410 AD. The Saxons took it over as a going concern and the mysterious Wessex dynasty (the Saxon leaders with British names) received the papal envoy Birinus here in 635. Christianity was already old in Britain and the name Wessex is derived from Gewisse, which could mean Gnostics rather than West Saxons. However, the baptism of King Cynegils here by St. Birinus was highly significant. This ancestor of King Alfred the Great granted land to Birinus in Dorchester for the establishment of a cathedral church and an episcopal see.

Dorchester was an odd choice for such an important function. It was too far north and this proximity to Mercia led to the bishopric being moved to Winchester. That's why, at the end of a long tale, there is only an abbey church here now (but well worth a visit, if only to see the Jesse window). Something was known about this place by the wise men who arranged such things as royal baptisms and cathedral sites. The ancient name of our premier river may provide a clue. The Romans latinized the British name for the river to 'Tamesis'. Early Saxon records have variants such as 'Thamisa'. The waterman poet John Taylor wrote a verse about Dorchester in 1632:

> *'There Tame and Isis doth*
> *embrace and kisse,*
> *Both joyn'd in one, cal'd Tame*
> *or Tame Isis'.*

Here we have it, if we would only look at the earth through the eyes of our ancient ancestors, who respected it as a living being. The river now commonly known as the Thames between its source (disputed, but officially near Kemble, in Gloucestershire) and Dorchester is actually the Isis. A few people in Oxford remembered this and braved the scorn of those who scoff at such things, by perpetuating this name on the Ordnance Survey maps and in the title of Oxford University Boat Club's second eight. Isis means Goddess, the Saviour Goddess par excellence who was potent as early as 3000 BC. Osiris was her brother and husband. They mated in the womb of their mother, the sky goddess Nuit. Possessor of the Ankh (symbol of divine authority and key to the house of life), she is represented by a throne in Egyptian hieroglyphs. The pharaohs were established on her throne, which shows her to be the power of the earth.

The cult of Isis declined only in name when Christianity was made the state religion of Rome. Her worship was transferred to the Blessed Virgin Mary. The statues of Isis suckling Horus became the models for the Madonna and Child. Mary inherited the role of Bride of God from Isis, while Isis' opposition to Set became Mary's opposition to Satan.

The River Isis is joined by the River Thame just south of Dorchester and below Castle Hill. When their waters mingle, they form the River Thames, or Thamesis (Thame-Isis). Thame is the male counterpart of the divine Wisdom of Isis. One function of Isis is to re-assemble lost knowledge. Note here that John Michell, the author of the seminal work 'New View Over Atlantis' (1983), traces a straight 'dragon' line or ley across southern Britain from near Land's End to the Norfolk Coast. It goes through such sacred places as Glastonbury Tor, Avebury and Bury St. Edmunds. It happens to cross the River Isis at Clifton Hampden, where St. Michael's Church stands on an astonishingly steep mound above the river two miles west of Dorchester and within the ancient sacred zone. St. Michael subdued the 'dragon', while this alignment of sacred sites is in line with sunrise on 1st May, Beltane. The dowser Hamish Miller has discovered male and female 'Michael' and 'Mary' energy lines coiled around this ley (see 'The Sun and the Serpent' by Miller and Broadhurst, 1989). Not knowing Oxfordshire or the Thames well, they missed the significance of their discovery that these male and female energy lines cross in the sacred grove or clump of trees on Castle Hill. This is directly above the confluence of the male River Thame and the female River Isis to form the River Thames – and where King Cynegils of Wessex was baptised.

Many have been inspired by this place. Look on the last tree on your right as you leave the clump on Castle Hill (going east). This is near a post numbered '2'. You can still make out a poem carved on it in 1847 by a member of the Tubb family:

'As up the hill with labouring steps we tread.
Where the twin clumps their sheltering branches spread,
The summit gained, at ease reclining stay,
And all around the wide-spread scene survey.
Point out each object, and instructive tell
The various changes that the land befell.
Where the low banks the country wide surround
The ancient earthwork formed old Mercia's bound.
In misty distance see the furrow heave
There lies forgotten lonely Gwichelm's grave.
Around the hill the ruthless Danes entrenched
And the fair plains with gory slaughter drenched.
While at our feet where stands that stately tower
In days gone by up rose Roman power.
And yonder there, where Thames' smooth waters glide,
In later days appeared monastic pride.
Within that field where lies the grazing herd
High walls were crumbled, stone coffins disinterred.
Such, in the course of time, is the wreck which fate
And awful doom award the earthly great'

The Walk

1. With your back to the Fleur De Lys Inn, go right up Rotten Row. At
the end of this cul-de-sac, turn right to follow a narrow path past
Blenheim Cottage on your left. Continue past allotments (on the site of
the Roman town). Follow the path as it goes left to pass cottages on your
right. Reach a road and go left along it for 100 yards. Bear right along
the public footpath signposted 'Day's Lock 3/4'. This is enclosed by
fences at first but then has a field on your right and leaves a garden
fence on your left behind to strike out ahead across a field towards the
impressive Iron Age earthworks called the Dyke Hills.

2. Turn right to follow the path past the Dyke Hills on your left.
Continue along a fenced track. Do not take the gate ahead at its end but
do bear left with the fenced path towards the river. Go through a gate
and bear slightly left across a field to the footbridge over the Isis near
Day's Lock, which is on your right. Cross the bridge, pass a box of 'Pooh
Sticks' on sale for the RNLI on your left, continue over two more bridges

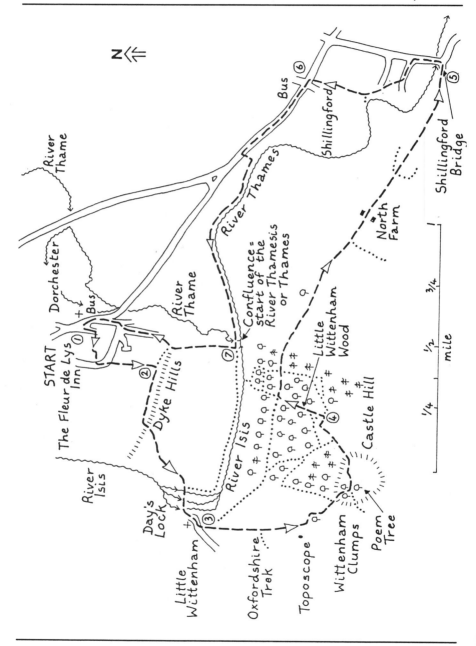

and along a road to see St. Peter's Church, Little Wittenham, on your right.

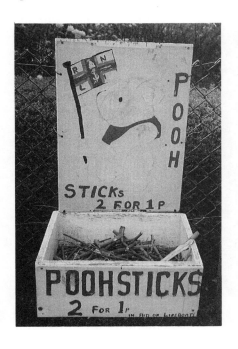

3. Turn left over a squeeze stile beside a gate into Little Wittenham Nature Reserve. Go ahead beside the hedge on your right towards the tree-topped Wittenham Clumps. Cross a stile beside a gate in the corner ahead. Go ahead, soon passing the way-marked stile beside a gate on your right which is used by the Oxfordshire Trek, and climb straight uphill. Admire the view from a toposcope on the top. Put the clump of trees on your right and aim for the next one, on Castle Hill. Cross a track going through a gate into the wood on your left. Go ahead over a way-marked stile in the next corner. Take steps down and up the hillfort's rampart. Go up to the clump of trees and enter by the way-marked path. Turn left at a path junction in this sacred grove. Pass a recumbent log with an information board about Castle Hill on it on your left. Emerge past the Poem Tree on your right, near a post numbered '2'. Descend to cut through the rampart past post '3'. Cross a stile beside a gate to pass post '4'. Walk beside a hedge on your left. Pass a stile beside a gate in it. Descend to the next gate on your left near a signpost in the bottom corner of the field.

4. Turn left through the gate and follow the woodland path downhill. Go around a barrier across it to reach a junction. Turn right along a wide bridleway. Emerge from the wood and Nature Reserve to follow the bridleway ahead between fields divided by a fence on your left. Continue past North Farm and reach Shillingford Bridge Hotel.

Descending from Castle Hill

5. Turn left over the bridge across the River Thames. Reach Ferry House on your right and turn left up the private road (but public footpath) opposite it. When this road forks, bear right through a metal kissing gate. follow the narrow path past Shillingford Court on your left and eventually reach a road.

6. Turn left along the pavement to pass the Kingfisher Inn on your left. Pass the bus stop, cross the road carefully and continue towards Dorchester on pavement. Pass a house called 'Thames Meadow' on your left. Go ahead 600 yards to a road sign pointing ahead to Dorchester. Turn left to cross the road with care and take a stile beside a gate into a meadow. This stile has lost its step, while the roadside signpost has lost its sign. There is a low way-mark post just inside the field. Go ahead to the river bank and turn right to walk upstream. Cross a bridge over the River Thame, overlooking its confluence with the Isis to form the Thames.

7. Turn right to walk with the River Thame on your right and across a meadow to a stile in the fence which divides it. Go ahead to pass the end of the Dyke Hills on your left and a World War II pill box on your right. Cross a stile and walk with a hedge on your right towards Dorchester. Go ahead along Wittenham Lane. Continue past St. Birinus' Roman Catholic chapel in Bridge End. Pass the Old Castle Inn on your left. Reach the main road opposite the abbey. Go left back to the Fleur de Lys Inn.

3|5|93

19. Christmas Common

Route: The Carvers Arms, Watlington – Pyrton Hill – The Fox and Hounds, Christmas Common – Lower Deans Wood – The Carvers' Arms, Watlington.

Distance: 5 miles.

Map: O.S. Pathfinder 1137 Watlington & Stokenchurch.

Park in free car park opp. pub .

Start: The Carvers' Arms, Watlington (Grid Reference SU 692944).

Not particularly nice pub.

Access: There is a reasonably good weekday bus service to Watlington from Oxford (No. 201). Yellow Bus (Tel. 0296 613831) run infrequent services to a galaxy of places, such as Henley, Reading, Wycombe and Aylesbury.

The Carvers' Arms, Watlington (049161 3470)

Children are welcomed by play equipment in the beer garden of this pub. Brakspear's real ales and bar snacks are available, while the restaurant is open on Wednesdays, Thursdays, Fridays and Saturdays, plus Sunday lunchtimes. The bar opening hours are 11 am to 11pm on weekdays, 12 noon to 3 pm and 7 pm to 10.30 pm on Sundays. There is a car par for patrons.

The Fox and Hounds Inn, Christmas Common (049161 2599)

Brakspear's real ales are served here too. This pub was built at least a century before the Civil War and the landlord can't remember any rival soldiers fraternising here on Christmas Day (1642,1643 or whenever). The bar snacks belong to the 20th century. Opening hours are 12 noon to 2.30 pm and 6 pm to 11 pm on weekdays, 12 noon to 2 pm and 7 pm to 10.30 pm on Sundays. There is a car park for patrons.

Beautiful pub run by old boy. We sat outside and enjoyed village life.

Christmas Common

Crossed by the Oxfordshire Way and overlooking the Ridgeway National Trail (here following the ancient Icknield Way), this is a mecca for ramblers. Beech trees and, in season, bluebells, grace the Chiltern uplands. There are splendid views over the Vale of Oxford. Watlington,

at the foot of the hill, dates from at least the 6th century. It obviously retains a medieval street plan. Once this may have been a border zone between Briton and invading Saxon, with a pub in Chapel Street being named the Black Horse. This could refer to King Arthur's knights (cf S. G. Wildman, 'The Black Horse Men', 1971). The Chilterns are surprisingly Celtic still. It seems the small, dark-haired, people survived here while the Saxons cleared the valleys.

This was a fighting zone during the Civil War. Royalists from Oxford were quartered here in April, 1642. Their presence wasn't permanent and the Roundheads held Watlington in July, 1643. The Royalists finally abandoned the place in February, 1644. Not before a curious myth was put abroad to explain the name of Christmas Common. Some say the rival armies were camped on opposite slopes when hostilities ceased because it was Christmas Day. No doubt someone produced a football . . . Can you really see Cromwell's men celebrating Christmas Day? The locals insist not. The name may come from an abundance of holly trees, known as Christmas trees. There was also a local family with the surname Christmas (but did they acquire it from the place they lived?). Do watch out for Santa's reindeer, however, including the small and shy muntjak deer from south-east Asia. Escapees from Woburn have found their way here.

* Fantastic woodland — bluebells as far as the eye could see. The path was short grass so walking made very easy. Best part of the walk.

The Walk

1. Go left along the pavement of Hill Road, towards the Chilterns. Pass Watlington Hospital on your right.

2. Turn left at the foot of the hill to take the signposted Ridgeway National Trail. Keep to the firm track, ignoring a signposted footpath crossing a stile on your right.

3. Turn at a crosstracks, leaving the Ridgeway for the signposted Oxfordshire Way Long Distance Path. Pass a sawmill and Pyrton Hill House on your right.

4. Fork right over a stile way-marked 'PY1' (Pyrton parish public footpath No. 1) as well as for the Oxfordshire Way. Bear right over a field to a way-marked stile in the opposite hedge. Do not cross it! Keep in the same field and go left to walk with the hedge on your right. Cross a stile in the corner and follow the hedge on your right to a road.

5. Turn right into Christmas Common. Go past the road down to Watlington on your right. Bear right at the fork ahead and come to the Fox and Hounds pub on your right.

6. With your back to the Fox and Hounds, go right to soon pass an Oxfordshire Way signpost on your left. Go ahead 100 yards and bear right along a lane signposted as a public footpath. After 150 yards, fork right off the lane to follow a grass path way-marked by a white arrow on a low post.

✱ 7. Follow this delightful woodland path which is way-marked by white arrows on trees. Continue through National Trust land at Lower Deans Wood. Ignore a stile in the perimeter fence on your right and follow the way-marked path just inside the edge of the wood.

8. Turn right, as way-marked, to a gate. Cross the stile to the right of it and go downhill to a lower gate. Follow a track through this and a belt of trees. Ignore turnings to left and right. Go ahead to the B481 road.

9. Turn right along the road for 300 yards. Turn right when the Ridgeway National Trail crosses the road. Go along this hedged track to the next road (Hill Road). Turn left along the pavement to retrace your steps to Watlington's Carvers' Arms Inn.

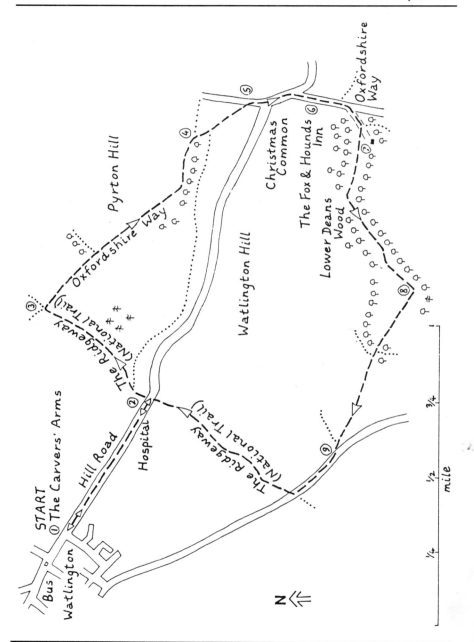

20. Wantage

Route: The Bell Inn, Wantage – East Lockinge – The Ridgeway – Letcombe Regis – The Bell Inn, Wantage.

Distance: 10 miles.

Map: O. S. Pathfinder 1154 Lambourn Downs and 1155 Harwell.

Start: The Bell Inn, Wantage (Grid Reference SU 398879).

Access: The Bell Inn is at the corner of the Market Square in Wantage, where there is ample car parking. Buses stop near King Alfred's Statue. These include the fast X31 direct from Oxford and the No. 31 from Oxford via Abingdon.

The Bell Inn, Wantage (02357 3718)

A ghost of a lady dressed in the style of the 18th century visits all the bedrooms here, so it doesn't matter which you choose should you need

bed and breakfast accommodation. Real ale and food are also available in this 17th century inn. There are underground tunnels from the cellars to the church and the bank. These hark back to the 'Black Wantage' (notorious for its lawless characters) of the early 19th century. If you want to enter by the conventional way, the pub is open from 11 am to 11 pm on weekdays and from 12 noon to 3 pm and between 7 pm and 10.30 pm on Sundays.

King Alfred's statue

King Alfred's Birthplace

Wantage is an ancient place, beside the Icknield Way and below the Ridgeway. The Romans settled here, while the Saxons chose it as a royal manor. Our greatest Saxon, King Alfred the Great, was born here in 849, the fourth son of Ethelwulf, King of Wessex. When they celebrated the millenium of his birth, a statue was commissioned. This was eventually erected in the market square in 1877 and bore a marked resemblance to Lord Wantage, Colonel Robert Lloyd-Lindsay VC KCB. Its inscription reads:

Alfred found learning dead, and he restored it:
Education neglected, and he revived it:
The laws powerless, and he gave them force:
The Church debased, and he raised it:
The land ravaged by a fearful enemy, from which he delivered it.

King Alfred's Way, a long distance walking route comes here on its 108 mile journey from Portsmouth (King Alfred is said to have founded the Royal Navy) and Winchester (Alfred's capital) to Oxford (where Alfred reputedly founded the University and his jewel is on display in the

Ashmolean Museum). The guide book to this route is by yours truly and is published by Thornhill Press. Robert Lloyd-Lindsay, Baron Wantage, won his Victoria Cross in the Crimean War. When he married Lord Overstone's daughter she brought him the largest estate of old Berkshire, exceeding 20,000 acres.

They became model estate owners, caring for their employees and 'always ready to play the part of benevolent friends to all who need their help'. His widow had a cross erected as a memorial to him in 1901, beside the Ridgeway and the route of this walk. It stands on an ancient tumulus and seems to mark where two leys cross (roughly north-south and east-west). Knowing the local stonemason, this was not a coincidence, as knowledge of the local leys has been handed down within his family for generations. Sadly, we can no longer travel to Wantage on the Tramway (initially horsedrawn) that connected it with the Great Western Railway mainline (Didcot – Swindon) at Wantage Road from 1875 to 1925 (passengers) and 1946 (goods).

The Walk

1. Cross Wantage's market square to pass King Alfred's statue on your right and go ahead along Wallingford Street, in the left hand corner ahead. Follow the pavement out of Wantage, passing Ormond Road on your right and Garston Lane on your left.

2. Turn right up Lark Hill for 300 yards. Turn left along a lane signposted as a public footpath to Lockinge (and part of the old Icknield Way). This soon deteriorates to a track. Join a minor road at its corner and go straight ahead. Turn right, then left with the road to enter East Lockinge.

3. Turn right at a T junction (towards Ginge). First, however, inspect the hut directly above it. This houses the old Lockinge fire engine. Pass Smith Cottage on your left, then pass parkland behind a wall on your left and a private drive on your left.

4. Turn right up a No Through Road. Pass the access drive to Lockinge Stud and Kitford on your left. Continue past Bitham Farm on your right.

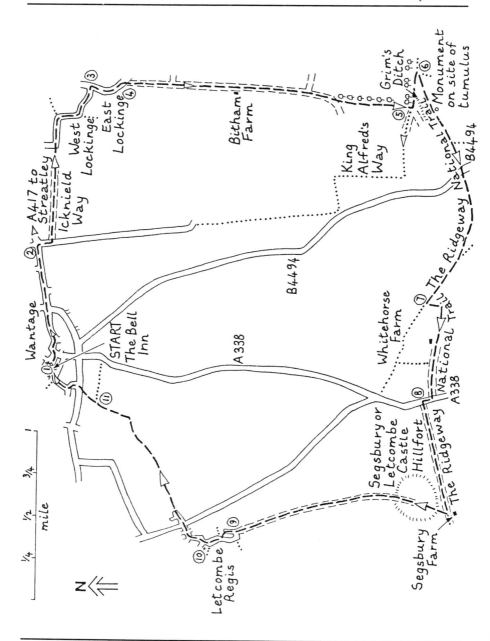

When the road turns left, go ahead up a rough lane way-marked as a footpath. When this bears right, go straight ahead up the signposted footpath and past a belt of trees on your left.

5. Turn left along a track which is way-marked as a bridleway. Pass a patch of woodland on your left. Cut across Grim's Ditch, evident on your right between two fields. This earthwork may pre-date or post-date the Romans. Admire the view over Oxfordshire on your left.

6. Turn sharply right along the Ridgeway. Ignore a track immediately on your left. Pass the monument to Robert Lloyd-Lindsay, Baron Wantage, VC KCB, on your left. Continue westwards with the Ridgeway, crossing the B4494 road.

7. Turn left with the signposted Ridgeway National Trail and follow the track which soon bears right to a road. Turn right along the road (the A338) for 200 yards.

8. Turn left to follow the Ridgeway, as signposted, past Redhouse Cottage on your right. Turn right along the track to Letcombe Castle (also known as Segsbury Castle) and follow the lane across the hillfort and down to Letcombe Regis.

9. When the road turn left, go ahead to pass The Sparrow pub on your left. Bear left along a path to pass Anvil Paddock on your right. Emerge at the road and go right along its elevated pavement.

10. Turn right opposite St. Andrew's Church. Follow the road towards Wantage, which soon bears left. Pass The Greyhound pub on your right, then turn right to a crossroads. Go ahead along the estate access road (Kings Close) which is signposted as the footpath to Wantage. Continue along a metalled path.

11. Reach a path junction and take the narrower route on your left. Emerge at a road (Portway) and cross it to go up Priory Road. Pass the church of SS Peter and Paul on your left. Turn left along Church Street, then turn right to the market square. Go left to return to The Bell, Wantage.

21. *Blewbury*

Route: The Red Lion Inn, Blewbury – Aston Tirrold – Chalk Hill Bottom
– The Ridgeway – Churn Rifle Range – The Red Lion Inn, Blewbury.

Distance: 9 miles.

Map: O.S. Pathfinder 1155 Harwell.

Start: The Red Lion Inn, Blewbury (Grid Reference SU 530857).

Access: Blewbury is on the A417 between Wantage and Streatley. There
is a bus service on Fridays only, run by Chiltern Queens (Tel. 0491
680354). Didcot, with its railway station providing frequent train services
to Oxford, is only 3 miles to the north, so if you rely on public transport,
allow plenty of time for a 15 mile ramble.

The Red Lion Inn, Blewbury (0235 850403)

This may have been where John Rothell and Osmund Brown were
reported for playing skittles on the Sabbath Day in 1590. The earliest
definite written record of the pub is in 1785, but it must be much older.
The locals are very keen on history, forming a Blewbury Local History
Group, so it wouldn't do for the landlord to advance dubious claims.
There is no doubt of the pub's ghost, however, with a recent witness of it
present when your author called in for a lemon and lime. It is quite
recent, being the Mrs. Tapp who was the licensee in the 1950s. She gave
herself a hard life running between the bar and the cellar, where she
kept her cash as well as the beer. She has been seen on the cellar steps
and has been known to knock glasses off shelves. Brakspear's real ale is
served, as well as bar snacks and meals. There is a beer garden and a car
park for patrons. The opening hours are 11 am to 2.30 pm and 6 pm to
11 pm from Mondays to Fridays, 11 am to 11 pm on Saturdays and 12
noon to 3 pm and 7 pm to 10.30 pm on Sundays.

The Red Lion

Blewbury

Call at Borlase, the antique shop in South Street (open on Sundays), to buy an excellent village history book (£2 in 1992). Entitled 'This Venerable Village' after its description as such in a Saxon charter, this is written by Peter Northeast, illustrated by Roy East and published by the Blewbury Local History Group. It shows how this place, with its thatched cottages and (reputedly Saxon) thatched walls, was once the most important settlement for some miles around. An estimated population of 400 in 1086 compares with a population of 623 recorded by the 1851 census. Spend awhile exploring its maze of paths to absorb a little of its character.

This is a special place which presumably came into being during Saxon times. The Ancient Britons had occupied the nearby hillfort of Blewburton, which may have been destroyed by the Romans when they invaded. Excavation has revealed evidence of violent destruction and burning. Perhaps the village is best known for its miserly curate, Morgan

Jones. He was here under John Keble, the father of the John Keble of Oxford Movement fame and also vicar of Coln St. Aldwyns near Fairford, from 1781 to 1824. Morgan Jones features in several books, including 'Our Mutual Friend' by Charles Dickens.

Although worth the considerable sum of £20,000, he wore the same hat and coat throughout his 43 year stay. He acquired a new brim for the hat from a scarecrow. He lived within his surplice fees of half a crown (12.5p) a week, surviving on bread, bacon and tea. His shirt was washed two or three times a month, while he gathered sticks from the churchyard for fuel. He once wrote a sermon on a marriage certificate and saved paper by writing another over the top of an earlier one, with the paper turned sideways. Churn rifle range was a popular tented army camp, with its own railway halt, before the first world war. St. Birinus, who was sent from Italy to baptise the Kings of Wessex, preached his first sermon on Churn Knoll in the seventh century.

The Walk

1. Go left from the Red Lion and take the footpath in the corner ahead, while the road bears right. Cross the Playclose (where the Maypole used to be erected). Take the hedged path ahead to St. Michael's Church. Pass the church on your right to leave the churchyard and turn right along an enclosed path which becomes Watt's Lane. Turn left at South Street for 150 yards.

2. Turn right along Besselslea Road to reach the B4016 to Didcot. Cross this carefully to maintain your direction along the signposted bridleway to Aston Upthorpe. This begins as a concrete farm access lane to pass Winterbrook Farm on your left but soon continues as a rough track. Pass Blewburton Hill, with its Iron Age hillfort, on your left. When the bridleway turns left at a crosstracks, go straight ahead along the signposted public footpath to Aston Tirrold.

3. Turn right along the road, soon passing a signposted bridleway on your left. Go ahead to cross the A417 (with care!) and take the 'No Through Road' ahead. Reach a fork in Chalk Hill Bottom and bear right. Pass a miniature railway in a garden on your right – there's a picture of

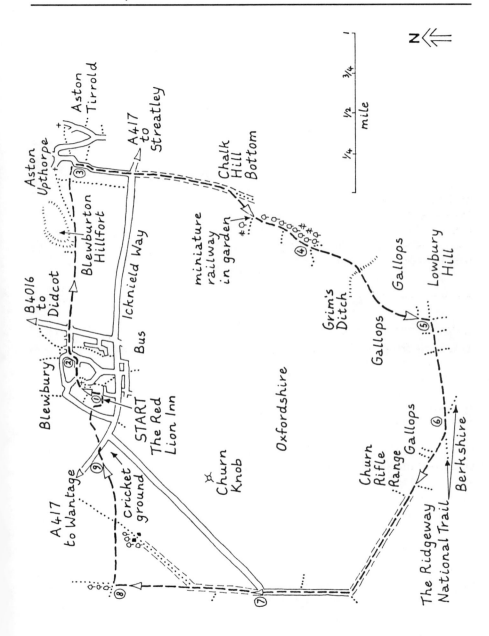

N

¼ ½ ¾
mile

Aston Tirrold

Aston Upthorpe

A417 to Streatley

③

Chalk Hill Bottom

Blewburton Hillfort

Icknield Way

Bus

miniature railway in garden

④

Grim's Ditch

Gallops

Lowbury Hill

Gallops

⑤

B4016 to Didcot

Blewbury

②

①

START
The Red Lion Inn

Oxfordshire

Churn Knob

Gallops

Churn Rifle Range

Gallops

⑥

Berkshire

A417 to Wantage

⑨

Cricket ground

The Ridgeway National Trail

⑧

⑦

this below. Go ahead towards the Downs, keeping to the main track
passing woodland on your left.

4. Climb with the main track to cut through Grim's Ditch (probably Iron
Age but possibly post-Roman). Pass training jumps for racehorses on
your right and follow the fenced track ahead. Note Lowbury Hill ahead
on your left. A Roman camp dating from the fourth century AD
occupied its summit. A large quantity of 1600 year old oyster shells
testify to the Roman diet.

5. Turn right at a crosstracks. Go ahead to join the Ridgeway National
Trail at a signpost. The heyday of this ancient route was as distant from
the Romans as they are from us.

6. Go right along the Ridgeway for 200 yards. Fork right just before the
next signpost, leaving the Ridgeway to head west to Uffington White
Horse, Avebury and the English Channel. Continue along a grass track
when a concrete farm access lane runs parallel to it on your right. Reach
a junction where a track goes left over a bridge across the dismantled

railway that was opened in 1882 to provide a through service from Southampton to the Great Western Railway at Didcot via Newbury. Sadly, this useful line was closed in 1964. Don't go over the railway bridge! Your way is right, along the metalled road. Pass a signposted bridleway on your right.

7. Leave the road when it bears right. Go straight ahead up a concrete farm access lane. When this concrete lane bears right, go straight ahead along a grass track. Notice the cooling towers of Didcot Power Station ahead. Reach the start of a hedge which runs along the left hand side of the track.

8. At the start of the hedge on your left, leave the track by turning right along a field path. This passes buildings encircled by trees on your right. Notice Wittenham Clumps on your left. Continue over a grass track descending from the buildings on your right. Go under a power line, bear left and pass under the power line again. Descend to a stile beside a signpost in the bottom corner of this field, near the cricket ground on your right.

9. Cross the stile to join the A417 road. Turn right for 50 yards, then turn left to cross the road carefully and take the signposted footpath ahead. Emerge in Westbrook Street, Blewbury. Go left for 20 yards, then turn right across the street and down a narrow, enclosed, footpath (Watery Lane). Emerge to pass Lawrence's Cottage (which has retained its name since a survey in 1548) on your right. Reach Chapel Lane and turn left to return to the Red Lion Inn.

22. *Wallingford*

Route: The George Hotel, Wallingford – Grim's Ditch – Upper House Farm – Carmel College – The George Hotel, Wallingford.

Distance: 10 miles.

Map: O.S. Pathfinder 1156 Henley-on-Thames.

Start: The George Hotel, Wallingford (Grid Reference SU 608895).

Access: Wallingford is served by the No. 390 bus between Oxford and London (daily) and the No. 5 bus between Oxford and Reading (weekdays only).

The George Hotel, Wallingford (0491 36665)

Non-residents are welcome in the Tavern Bar, which is open from 10 am to 2.30 pm and 6 pm to 11 pm Mondays to Fridays, 10 am to 2.30 pm and 7 pm to 11 pm on Saturdays, and 12 noon to 3 pm plus 7 pm to 10.30 pm on Sundays. Usher's real ale is served while there is a fine restaurant. If you need accommodation, have the courage to stay overnight in the Tear-drop Room. It could lead to a midnight rendezvous with the inn-keeper's daughter. Unfortunately, she is a sad ghost of a girl who died over 300 years ago. Many have heard or seen her, more have felt a presence and been moved to pity her.

Royalist soldiers were billeted here during the Civil War. They were so rowdy that a gibbet was erected in the town square to give instant capital punishment to any soldier caught fighting in the town at night. The innkeeper at the George, a Mr. Smith, was also under threat from the authorities for brewing his own beer. The local Justices of the Peace were dealing with Smith when his beautiful daughter was to keep a date with a handsome Royalist sergeant, John Hobson. Distracted by the J.P.s, the innkeeper and his daughter were not in the bar when some local ruffians picked a quarrel with Sergeant Hobson. Mindful of the gibbet, Hobson was unable to adequately defend himself in a fight. One of the ruffians stabbed and mortally wounded him. By the time Smith and his daughter arrived on the scene, Hobson lay dying in a pool of blood. His beautiful lover screamed and screamed. She then took to her room, out of her mind with grief. For the rest of her short life, she stayed there and mixed soot from the fireplace with her tear-drops. She drew beautiful tear-drop shapes all over her bedroom wall and constantly whispered John Hobson's name. Eventually her strength left her and she died of lost love. Some of her tear-drops remain, however, to be seen by guests staying in her old room.

One man booked in for the night at the end of the 19th century without knowing the room's history. He awoke to an early morning thunderstorm. The flashes of lightning silhouetted a young girl tracing tear-drop shapes on the wall. When she turned to face him, he saw a beautiful girl dressed in a white shroud and with black hair tumbling down her shoulders. Her face was pale and lonely, with wild, sad, eyes. Tears trickled mournfully down her cheeks. Going back to sleep, the man woke up much later convinced he'd been dreaming. Then he saw a scattering of soot on the floor near the wall where the girl had stood. On the wall itself were fresh, black, tear-drops. He called the landlord who, after hearing the traveller's tale, told him of the room's history. Her ghost was last seen in 1977. Dick Turpin also frequented this inn, using a room over the courtyard, while ghostly noises have been heard in the cellar late at night. Measured footsteps prowling the corridors at night are not unusual.

Wallingford

History has been made here. Who now knows the story of the Icknield Way, which forded the Thames at Wallingford? The Romans most probably fortified the crossing and there may have been a heroic struggle here between Britons and Saxons in the Dark Ages. It was the tyrant and usurper to the British throne, Vortigern, who invited Hengist and Horsa here and later became infatuated with Rowena. As a child, I remember learning that a sweet-shop in Wallingford used to be called Vertigern's. Could there be a connection?

The Saxons certainly valued the place, erecting defensive ramparts and locating the royal mint here. The Normans wasted no time in securing it with a mighty castle. This guarded a bridge which was definitely there in 1141 and was most probably referred to in writing in 957. Wallingford played an important role in the civil war between Stephen and Matilda. The castle provided the queen with refuge when she escaped from Oxford along the frozen Thames, then it was the scene of the signing of the Treaty of Wallingford which brought hostilities to a conclusion in 1154. The new King Henry II granted the town its charter in 1155. Gardens occupy the site of the castle today. Its stone was used to repair Windsor Castle in the 16th century. Despite this it withstood a Parliamentary siege for 65 days during the Civil War and became one of the last Royalist centres to surrender. Cromwell feared it so much that he ordered the castle to be demolished. Come on an afternoon (not Sundays or Mondays) in the summer and you can still visit the Wallingford Museum, however. This is housed in Flint House in the High Street (Tel. 0491 35065).

The Walk

1. With your back to the George Hotel, go left along Watlington's High Street. Pass Castle Lane on your left. Go ahead over the bridge. Turn right along a muddy lane just before Bridge Villa International Camping and Caravan Park.

2. Ignore a kissing gate beside a fieldgate ahead. Bear left with the enclosed track. Reach a track junction and go right along a concrete farm access lane for 10 yards. Turn left over a way-marked stile to follow a clear path across the corner of the field. Continue through a gap in the hedge to the far right corner of the next field. Emerge at the A4074 beside a Ridgeway signpost.

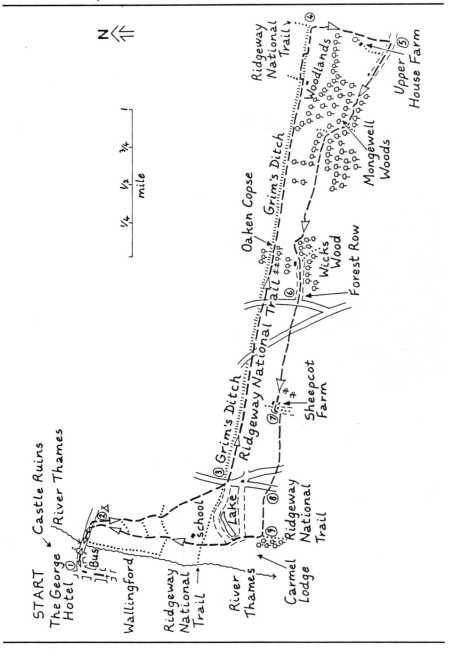

The Ridgeway, following Grim's Ditch

3. Cross the road with care and, opposite an entrance of Carmel College, go ahead along the signposted Ridgeway. This follows Grim's Ditch (probably Iron Age, possibly post Roman). Go ahead across two lanes. Oaken Copse is a place to come for bluebells in season. Pass a house (Woodlands) on your right. Eventually come to a signpost at a path T junction.

4. Turn right, away from the Ridgeway National Trail. Cross a stile to follow a woodland path. Continue beside a fence on your left and along the edge of a field ahead. Cross an iron ladder stile in the next corner. Skirt woodland to leave it by a wooden step stile next to a signpost. Take the enclosed path ahead and continue down the farm access lane.

5. Turn right along a road. This passes a duck pond on your right and becomes a rough track. Continue through Mongewell Woods. Go ahead beside a fence on your right. Bear right, as way-marked, around Wicks Wood. Reach a lane at Forest Row.

6. Cross the lane and go ahead up a track. Soon cross a second lane and go ahead along the signposted bridleway. This crosses fields to Sheepcot

Farm. Follow the concrete access lane around a bend to pass the farmhouse on your left.

7. Turn right to follow a fence on your right along the edge of a field. Go through a gate in the corner to the A4074. Go right along the grassy verge for 50 yards then turn left carefully across the road. Continue through a small wooden gate beside a public bridleway signpost. Descend with the fence on your right. Take the signposted gap in the corner. Turn right along the road for 20 yards.

8. Turn left down a signposted path. Cross the stile in the fence below the road. Bear right with a wooden fence and walk down the edge of this field beside the fence on your right. Go ahead through a gate in the next corner. Cross a narrow field to a stile beside a gate. Go ahead to a firm track.

9. Turn right along a track to pass woodland on your left. Follow the drive through Carmel College. Pass a lake on your right. When the drive bends right, go ahead up the way-marked (and paved) bridleway. When the Ridgeway National Trail turns right over a way-marked stile, go straight ahead to keep with the bridleway. Continue over a stile, pass farm buildings on your left and houses on your right. Maintain your direction over a stile beside a gate and along a meadow. Cross another stile beside a gate ahead. Follow the fence on your left. Go through a kissing gate and bear left to a road. Go left to retrace your steps into Wallingford.

23. *Stonor*

Route: The Rainbow Inn, Middle Assendon – Bix Bottom – Maidens-grove – Stonor – Coxlease Farm – The Rainbow Inn, Middle Assendon.

Distance: 6 miles.

Map: O.S. Pathfinder 1156 Henley-on-Thames.

Start: The Rainbow Inn, Middle Assendon (Grid Reference SU 738858).

Access: There is an infrequent bus service (Yellow Bus) between Henley and Watlington via Middle Assendon and Stonor. It is worth considering if you are to travel from (and back to) Watlington (which has buses from and to Oxford) on a Thursday. Check first with Oxfordshire County Council (0865 810405). Another way would be to link this walk with route 26 (Henley-on-Thames). Henley is easy to reach by public transport and the two routes join at the Rainbow Inn, Middle Assendon, to give a 13 mile walk. Cars can be parked by patrons at the Rainbow Inn, which is on the B480 between Henley and Watlington.

The Rainbow Inn, Middle Assendon (0491 574879)

The local Brakspear's real ales are served here, as are bar meals. This is a very old pub, dating from the 15th century. Opening times are 11 am to 2.30 pm and 6 pm to 11 pm on weekdays, 12 noon to 3 pm and 7 pm to 10.30 pm on Sundays.

The Stonor Arms Hotel, Stonor (0491 63345)

This is no longer a pub! Real ale is available in the bar and it is a worthy local – Old Luxtor's barn ale from Chiltern Valley Winery near Turville Heath. Drinks are only served to non-residents who buy a meal in the restaurant, however. A bowl of soup cost £3.15 in 1992. As the restaurant may be booked by wedding parties, do telephone ahead. Bed and

breakfast is also available (£82.20 single, £92.50 double per night in 1992). The restaurant is open from 11.45 am to 1.45 pm and from 6.45 pm to 9.30 pm daily. There is a car park for patrons.

Stonor

Time your trip well to combine this walk with a visit to Stonor House and Park. From April to September inclusive this is possible on every Sunday afternoon (2 – 5.30 pm) and on Bank Holiday Mondays. Between May and September you can also visit on Wednesday afternoons, while in July and August it is possible to visit on Thursday afternoons as well. If you want to come on a Saturday afternoon this is alright in August only. There is an admission fee. Telephone 049163 587 for further details.

The House has a Georgian front but is mostly medieval. The same family has lived in it since the 12th century, but their decision not to rebuild between the 16th century and the 18th century was forced upon them by circumstances.

The Stonors were Roman Catholics and paid heavy penalties for their beliefs after the Reformation. They didn't make life easy for themselves when they hid the Jesuit priest Edmund Campion in a secret room in their house. Here he supervised the printing of his ten reasons for being a Roman Catholic, 'Decem Rationes'. 400 copies were distributed at the degree – giving ceremony in St. Mary's Church, Oxford, on 27th June, 1681. With the Spanish Armada only seven years away, this action soon led to Campion's arrest, torture and execution. The House contains an exhibition about Campion's life and work. The Park is famous for its deer. You may well see some under the trees near the road with others on the hills beyond. Male fallow deer shed their antlers and grow new ones each year. These reach their full size in the eighth year. Scabs can be seen in the spring where the antlers have been shed. The young antlers begin to make branches in July and reach full size in August. Their protective skin is then shed in bloody strips to leave pristine antlers.

The Walk

1. With your back to the Rainbow Inn, go left. Ignore the first turn on your left, but take the second. This is signposted to Bix Bottom. Keep right at a junction with a road coming from your left. This route is now part of the Oxfordshire Cycleway (as well as being on the Oxfordshire Way long distance path). Pass a signposted footpath on your left, just before the ruins of the old St. James' Church. The hamlet of Bix has moved and the new parish church is passed on route 26 (Henley-on-Thames).

2. Turn right up a hedged track (signposted as the Oxfordshire Cycleway). Continue through the woodland of Warburg Nature Reserve. Go ahead with the way-marked Oxfordshire Way (notice the letters 'OW' on the blue arrow). Pass a signposted stile on your left, just before Lodge Farm.

3. Take the lane ahead. This bends right at Maidensgrove. Don't go left with a second bend. Go straight ahead along the signposted path in the corner. Continue over a way-marked stile and cross a field to the woodland ahead. Pass a pond on your right and enter the wood at the way-marked gap. Turn left along the way-marked path PS17, here part of the Oxfordshire Way.

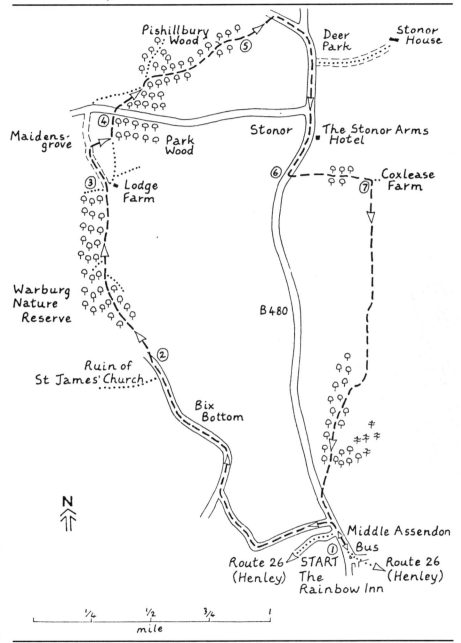

Pishillbury Wood ⑤

Deer Park

Stonor House

Maidens-grove ④

Park Wood

Stonor

The Stonor Arms Hotel

⑥ ⑦ Coxlease Farm

③ Lodge Farm

B 480

Warburg Nature Reserve

② Ruin of St James' Church

Bix Bottom

N

Middle Assendon

Bus

Route 26 (Henley)

START ① The Rainbow Inn

Route 26 (Henley)

¼ ½ ¾ 1
mile

4. Cross a road to go ahead along the signposted Oxfordshire Way. This soon bears right. It is joined by a path from your left. Go ahead to a way-marked fork and bear right along path PS9. Follow this path's white way-mark arrows through the wood.

5. Go ahead down a hedged path to the B480 road. Turn right into Stonor. Pass the entrance to Stonor Park and House on your left. Continue past the Stonor Arms Hotel.

6. Turn left over a stile to follow the signposted footpath beside a fence on your left to a stile in the top corner. Go ahead through woodland to Coxlease Farm.

7. Turn right along a track which eventually bears right down to a wood. Go left along a woodland path. Bear right down a track to the B480 road. Turn left back to Middle Assendon, where the Rainbow Inn is on your right.

24. Uffington White Horse

Route: The Rose and Crown, Ashbury – Ridgeway – Wayland's Smithy – Uffington White Horse – Woolstone -Compton Beauchamp – The Rose and Crown, Ashbury.

Distance: 7^1/$_2$ miles.

Map: O.S. Pathfinder 1154 Lambourn Downs.

Start: The Rose and Crown Inn, Ashbury (Grid Reference SU 265851).

Access: Take the train to Swindon for the good weekday bus service (No. 47) to Ashbury run by Thamesdown Transport (Tel. 0793 523700 for timetable information). Most buses go between Swindon and Newbury (sometimes requiring a change to a Bee Line bus at Lambourn). Some buses run to Woolstone on Saturdays. Wiltshire County Council have done a lot to promote public transport, including this service.

The No. 47 is ideal for Ridgeway walkers, so please do use it. Although Ashbury is just inside Oxfordshire, you can travel here on a Wiltshire Day Rover. This bargain ticket is issued and accepted on dozens of bus companies in Wiltshire and surrounding counties. Oh, for such council-inspired co-operation between the rival bus companies in Oxfordshire! You can actually buy a Wiltshire Day Rover on Swindon and District bus No. 66 from Oxford to Swindon and change there for a journey to Ashbury on the No. 47 at no extra charge. The connections aren't good and you won't have time for all of this walk, however. The train ride between Didcot and Swindon is recommended for its view of the White Horse. It is possible to take the No. 66 bus from Oxford to Faringdon and change there to bus No. 68 on Fridays (except public holidays) only. Take this No. 68 to the White Horse Inn in Woolstone and start this circuit at point 6. If you don't think you'll make it for the return bus, halt at point 1 to bus back from Ashbury. Return on another Friday to walk from Ashbury back to the bus stop in Woolstone. Telephone 0793 522243 for the No. 66 and 68 bus times.

The Rose and Crown Inn, Ashbury (0793 710222)

Real ale is served in this pub which is a popular bed and breakfast stop for Ridgeway walkers. Food is available and there is a car park for patrons. Opening hours are 11.30 am to 2.30 pm and 6.30 pm to 11 pm from Mondays to Fridays, 11 am to 2.30 pm and 6.30 pm to 11 pm on Saturdays, plus 12 noon to 3 pm and 7 pm to 10.30 pm on Sundays.

The White Horse Inn, Woolstone (036782 566)

Bed and breakfast is available in this pub too. Bombardier is one of the real ales on offer, while food can be served. Opening hours are 11 am to 3 pm and 6 pm to 11 pm on weekdays, 12 noon to 3 pm and 7 pm to 10.30 pm on Sundays. Thomas Hughes is said to have written 'Tom Brown's School Days' here in 1856. The school Tom Brown (but not Thomas Hughes) attended is in a corner of the churchyard at nearby Uffington, where Hughes lived as a young child. The school was built in 1617 but this inn pre-dates it.

A Sacred Pilgrimage

Not much evidence of humanity pre-dates the Ridgeway. This is the classic section of Our Oldest Road, culminating in one of the finest views in England from Uffington White Horse. This was more than an artery for trade or a marching route for armies to our distant ancestors. This was a powerful living entity, bringing vitality to all. Walk here as a pilgrim, respect the holy places and absorb the atmosphere. G. K. Chesterton gave expression to it in his 'Ballad of the White Horse':

> 'Before the gods that made the gods,
> Had seen their sunrise pass,
> The White Horse of the White Horse Vale,
> Was cut out of the grass.'

What is this beast? Who made it, when and why? Now in the care of English Heritage, it is 360 feet long and 160 feet high. It is also best seen from the air, or at least several miles away in the valley. This prompts thoughts as to who was meant to see it and how did they manage to cut it so accurately? Cut it they did, and scour it regularly to maintain its outline in the chalk. Thomas Hughes wrote of the last traditional scouring, in 1857. There were great festivities, including cheese-rolling down the Manger. The locals attributed it to King Alfred the Great, who defeated the Danes in the Battle of Ashdown, which was fought near here in 870. This was typical. They could identify with Alfred and give him credit for the deeds of long forgotten heroes. Iron Age currency bars link it with the Dubunni tribe. Perhaps it was their tribal badge, aimed to impress those stuck in the valley. They would have been precious few because the Romans were probably the first to tackle the dense forests of the clay vale. The Britons preferred the chalk hills, where the prehistoric trackway ran.

The Icknield Way provided a parallel fine-weather route at the foot of the chalk linking the 'Spring line villages' on a narrow band of green

sand, but the White Horse stood more chance of impressing a Martian in a flying saucer than people on the Icknield Way. It is there because it is there. It has probably been there for aeons, adopted by successive invaders (if the original population ever were removed). It could have become Alfred's badge just as Arthur became the national hero of the very English he had fought against. It may not be a horse. It may be a dragon.

The Ridgeway

Guy Underwood, the dowser, wrote in 'Pattern of the Past' (1969) that there were two figures – a dragon and a horse. A horse would be appropriate for the Celtic goddess Rhiannon (the Roman Epona), representing the fertility of the land. Dragons personify the life force, especially when it needs to be controlled by a dragon-slayer. Who better than St. George? The seemingly artificial mound below the horse or dragon is called Dragon Hill. This is where George slew the dragon. There are a couple of bald patches on the hill's flat top to prove it. These are inexplicably bare of grass (and were in previous centuries, according to old pictures). They were scorched by the dragon's blood. Guy Underwood (*op.cit.*) dowsed blind springs marking terminations of right-handed multiple spirals – 'A phenomenon of great rarity and sanctity'. Kenneth Grahame set his story 'The Reluctant Dragon' here. Of course, nowadays we must echo John Aubrey's words of 1687:

'To save a mayd St. George the Dragon slew-
A pretty tale, if all is told be true.
Most say there are no dragons, and 'tis sayd
There was no George, pray God there was a mayd.'

There is a ley (dragon line?) according to Paul Devereux in his 'The Ley Hunter's Companion' (1979). Running for some 10 miles from Berkshire, it links Uffington Castle, Dragon Hill and St. Mary's Church, Uffington. Another ley has been put forward linking the White Horse with the Rollright Stones in the very north of Oxfordshire. Uffington Castle is an Iron Age hillfort (one of several along the Ridgeway and linked to pressure from immigrants coming this way around 300 BC). Before descending from its 855 ft viewpoint, stand in the eye of the horse, shut your eyes, turn round three times in a clockwise direction and make a wish. Guy Underwood found a powerful blind spring at this spot too! It traditionally brings good luck.

If it is a horse, it could have had its feet shod at Wayland's Smithy. Experts say horses didn't bother with shoes in the very old days. They also make Wayland the Smith out to be a latecomer, imported from Scandinavia. Nevertheless it's his name on the signpost pointing to the ancient long barrow. This is nearly 200 feet long, 50 feet wide and has 10 feet high sarsen stones at its mouth. It also dates back to 3700 BC and was enlarged by 3400 BC. Fourteen skeletons were found in the original barrow and eight more in the extension.

The story is that if you leave your horse and a coin here and go away for a while, the horse will have new shoes and your coin will have disappeared upon your return. The Smith has featured in Sir Walter Scott's 'Kenilworth' (1821) and Rudyard Kipling's 'Puck of Pook's Hill' (1906).

In Norse mythology, Wayland is a smith of supernatural skill. He was captured by a king and made lame to prevent escape. Set to work, the smith gained revenge by killing the king's two young sons and making cups from their skulls. He then raped the king's daughter and escaped by magically flying through the air. Wayland is actually better known for making gold cups than shoeing horses. Above all he was a magician. The tale of paying for a service that is done in secret is a theme well-known to children (cf 'The Elves and the Shoemaker'). Some say Wayland was an elf.

Wayland's Smithy lies beside the Ridgeway. This official National Trail was opened as an 85 mile route between Overton Hill and Ivinghoe Beacon in 1973. The ancient Ridgeway can be traced for some 300 miles between Devon and Norfolk. An unofficial long distance path of 64 miles now terminates at Wayland's Smithy. It crosses Oxfordshire from Wormleighton Reservoir on the Oxford Canal and is named the d'Arcy Dalton Way after a man who gave 50 years service to the cause of rights of way in Oxfordshire. Fittingly, it visits the old church below Wayland's Smithy at Compton Beauchamp. This is dedicated to (founded by?) St. Swithin. He was Welsh and his name means magician, shaman or Druid in Welsh. He was famous for influencing the weather.

The Wessex kings were strongly influenced by the Welsh (giving credence to their name, Gewisse, meaning Gnostics rather than West Saxon). King Ethelwulf made Swithin Bishop of Winchester in 852. When he died in 862 he was buried outside the cathedral, in druid fashion. In 971, his body was removed inside, on the famous 15th July, when we all know that if it rains there will be 40 more days of rain to follow. Even the name Compton is a Celtic influence, being Cwm Tun (valley hamlet).

The Walk

1. Go right, past the bus shelter. Turn right up the B4000 towards Lambourn. Turn right along a track signposted as 'Public Footpath: The Ridgeway $1/2$'. Turn left with this path to walk uphill with the church at your back.

2. Turn left along the Ridgeway. Follow this ancient, broad, track across the B4000 and over a crosstracks. Look for Wayland's Smithy, guarded by tall trees on your left. Take a gate to divert left along a fenced path to visit it.

3. Continue eastwards along the Ridgeway. Ignore a lane to Compton Beauchamp on your left. Head for Uffington Castle, whose earthworks are on the skyline. Go over a crosstracks, and pass a stile giving access to National Trust land on your left. Pass a signposted bridleway on your right.

4. Turn left over a stile beside a gate. Visit Uffington Castle and bear right to the White Horse. Descend to a road and climb Dragon Hill on the other side. Bear slightly left as you descend. Cross a stile in the fence ahead and continue down to the B4507 road (the Icknield Way).

5. Turn left along the road, then turn right down to Woolstone. Pass the turning to All Saints Church on your right. Go left to the White Horse Pub, Woolstone.

6. With your back to the pub, go left along the lane. When this bends right, go straight ahead along the way-marked public footpath. Cross the stile into the field and walk beside the hedge on your left. Take a stile in the corner, soon followed by a second stile, continue beside a hedge on your left in the next field and cross the stile in its corner.

7. Turn left along a raised path and almost immediately ignore a path going to a footbridge and a gate on your right. Go ahead a few more yards, then take the next path on your right. Pass through woodland and cross a footbridge near the corner of a ditch. Continue beside a fence on your right. Keep it there over two more fields.

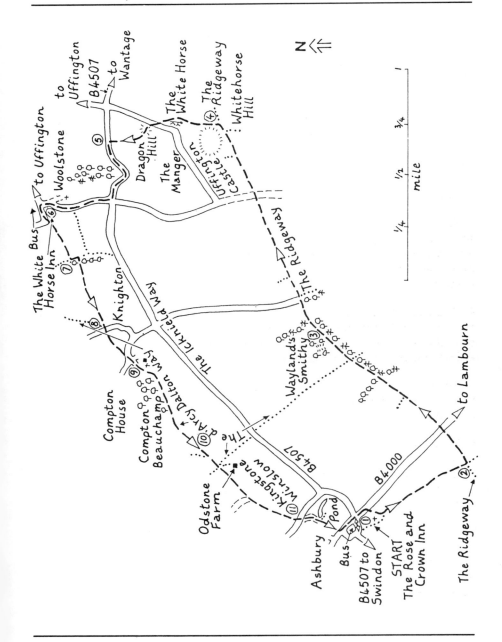

8. Cross a road at Knighton. Take the signposted bridleway through a gate ahead. Follow the fence on your left to a way-marked gate ahead. Continue along a track to a road. Bear right into Compton Beauchamp. As the road bends right, go straight ahead up the lane, passing Compton House on your left. Approach St. Swithin's Church.

9. Visit the church and go left from it through the gate beside a signpost. Follow the path towards Kingstone Winslow. Pass a dovecote on your left and take the gate in the fence ahead. Bear right to pass a jutting corner of woodland on your right and go through a gate in the fence ahead. Cross a field to the gap in its corner. Continue with a hedge on your left. Eventually drop down to a footbridge with a d'Arcy Dalton Way way-mark. Cross into the next field.

10. Go ahead to pass Odstone Farm on your left and cross a field to a stile in its corner. Cross it and follow the hedge on your left until a track junction. Go ahead over a stile and follow the fence on your left until a gate. Turn left through this to reach a road in Kingstone Winslow.

11. Go left and fork right down a No Through Road. Pass a duckpond on your left. Take the signposted and metalled bridleway ahead to Ashbury. Turn left along the pavement to the crossroads. Turn right to the bus shelter and the Rose and Crown.

25. The Maharajah's Well

Route: The Cherry Tree Inn, Stoke Row – Homer Cottage – Garsons Farm – Scot's Farm – The Maharajah's Well – The Cherry Tree Inn, Stoke Row.

Distance: 6 miles.

Map: O.S. Pathfinder 1156 Henley-on-Thames.

Start: The Cherry Tree Inn, Stoke Row (Grid Reference SU 683841).

Access: There is an infrequent bus service to Stoke Row from Reading, run by Chiltern Queen Coaches and Bee Line. Telephone 0734 581358 for times. Patrons may park their cars at the Cherry Tree Inn.

The Cherry Tree Inn (0491 680430)

Brakspear's real ale is served in this pub. Children are welcome to play on the equipment in the beer garden, which is brightened by the survivors of a cherry orchard. Bar snacks are available. Prince Philip dined here in 1964, when the Maharajah's Well celebrated its centenary. Opening hours are 11 am to 3 pm and 6 pm to 11 pm on weekdays, 12 noon to 3 pm and 7 pm to 10.30 pm on Sundays.

The Maharajah's Well

This must be the most unexpected sight in an Oxfordshire village. Stoke Row's well is topped by a distinctively Indian Construction. Around 1850 a Mr. Edward Anderson Reade, who was soon to be appointed Lieutenant-Governor of the North-Western Provinces of India, discussed the common problem of water shortage shared by the Benares area and the Chiltern village of Stoke Row with the Maharajah of Benares. Mr. Reade's father's estates were at Stoke Row, where villagers collected rain water for cooking. Pond water was used for washing, while drinking water was a precious commodity in dry weather.

The Maharajah's Well

Events such as the Indian Mutiny intervened, but the Maharajah determined to make a gift of a well to Stoke Row as a token of his friendship. Digging started on the future King Edward VII's wedding day, 10th March, 1863. It was a massive task for hand labour, working at a width of only four feet and going down 368 feet – more than twice the height of Nelson's Column. The water was actually 342 feet down but the extra depth allowed for seasonal fluctuations.

The water was also drawn up by hand, with two narrow-topped nine gallon buckets counter balancing each other. Even a woman or a young boy could turn a handle and draw up a full bucket in only 10 minutes. The water was then transferred to other containers and carried to the cottages. Sometimes a horse drawn cart was available. Mr. Reade designed the superstructure and took a photograph of it for the Maharajah.

The well was officially opened on Queen Victoria's birthday, 24th May, 1864. A warden was housed in a specially-built cottage. The Maharajah wanted the water to be provided to the public for free, so the well, warden and cottage were maintained by the profits from a cherry orchard which the Maharajah also paid to establish. When the Prince of Wales recovered from typhoid in 1872, the Maharajah gave the village £200 to celebrate. Each household received half a pound of tea, one pound of sugar, two loaves of bread, two pounds of bacon and a pair of blankets. The gentlemen and yeomen ate a lunch at the Cherry Tree Inn, then acted as waiters for a lunch for 150 labourers, served in a specially built shed. The women and children had a tea party in the schoolroom. Sports and a firework display followed. Mains water arrived in 1906 and more reliably in 1927, but a few villagers relied on the well up to 1939.

The Walk

1. Go right from the Cherry Tree Inn. Go ahead at the crossroads and past the Farmers Inn on your right. Turn right along Cox's Lane. Pass the access to Stoke Row Farm on your right. Continue along an old green lane until it reaches a road. Cross this to take the lane ahead, signposted for 'Homer only'.

2. Reach Homer Cottage on your left and turn left immediately after it, crossing a stile beside a gate next to a signpost. Bear right to pass a fenced and tree-ringed dried-up pond, then go left across pasture to a stile giving access to a wood. Follow the path ahead just inside the edge of this wood. Cross a muddy farm track and continue to descend through woodland. Join a lower track.

3. Turn right along the lower track. Maintain your direction past Lower Handsmooth Farm on your left. After the next house (Headlams Farm), turn left along the signposted footpath. Go up the field close to the right hand hedge. Cross a stile into woodland near the top corner.

4. Climb through the trees to the top of a ditch. Turn right along a raised path through trees to reach a road. Go right down the road. Take the first way-marked footpath on your left. This bears sharply left to cross a field diagonally to a stile in its far left corner. Maintain your direction over pasture, across a way-marked stile and along a woodland path. Merge with a path coming from your right near the corner of a wood. Continue with the edge of the wood on your right. Look for a stile in its perimeter fence.

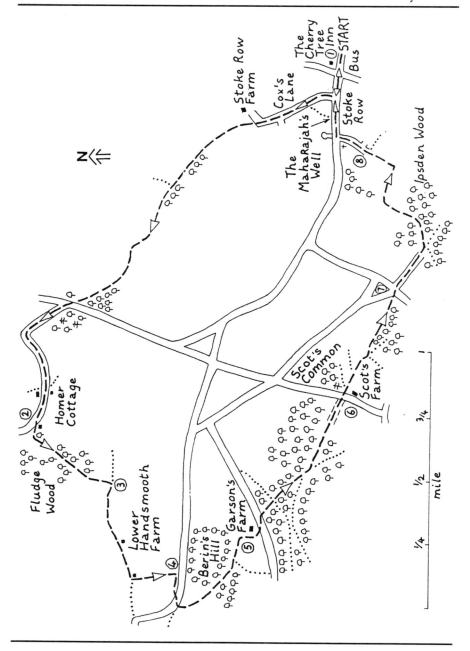

5. Turn right over a stile and walk away from the wood, keeping a fence on your right. Go over a stile to a road. Turn left for 75 yards, passing Garson's Farm on your left. Turn right down a woodland path. Cross a lower track and climb ahead. Pass houses on your right and reach a minor road at Scot's Farm.

6. Cross the road and pass an ancient oak tree on your right. Continue past a barn on your right. Keep to the firm track past woodland on your left. Pass an enchanting pink cottage on your left, cross a stile beside a fieldgate ahead. Don't go ahead through a gate into a wood, but do go left through a gap and turn right to walk along the field past the wood on your right. Cross a stile beside a gate ahead to reach a minor road.

7. Ignore the lane on your left, cross the minor road and take the lane ahead. Pass a house on your right and turn left at the edge of a wood. Follow the way-marked path. This leads through the wood to pass a farm on your right. Follow the fenced path across a field on your right. Go left along a track into Stoke Row. Take the road ahead, passing St. John the Evangelist's Church on your left. Turn right at the main road. Pass Church View on your left, then come to the Maharajah's Well on your left. Go ahead to pass Cox's Lane on your left and retrace your steps to the Cherry Tree Inn.

26. Henley-on-Thames

Route: The Angel on the Bridge Inn, Henley – Lambridge Wool – Bix – Middle Assendon – Henley Park – The Angel on the Bridge Inn, Henley.

Distance: 7 miles.

Map: O. S. Pathfinder 1156 Henley-on-Thames.

Start: The Angel on the Bridge Inn, Henley (Grid Reference SU 763826).

Access: Henley is easy to reach by public transport. Salter Bros. run steamer trips to here from Reading and Marlow. Telephone 0865 243421 for details. British Rail has a branch line from Twyford to Henley. If you're coming from Oxford, the most convenient way would be on Oxford Tube's No. 390 bus (daily service). There are other buses from places like Reading, Wycombe and Watlington.

The Angel on the Bridge Inn, Henley (0491 410678)

Drink the local Brakspear's real ale and eat a meal on the picturesque river terrace. Opening times are 11 am to 11 pm on weekdays, 12 noon to 3 pm and 7 pm to 10.30 pm on Sundays. The Angel vies with the Little Angel on the Berkshire side of the bridge as the authentic location of a dramatic moment in Henley's history. Mary Blandy stood to inherit a fortune when she murdered her father by poisoning his food with arsenic on 14th August, 1751. The arsenic was provided by her lover, a Scottish soldier who was unacceptable to Mr. Blandy, a successful Solicitor, because he already had a wife and child in Scotland. The deluded Mary believed the powder to be a love potion. When the doctor became suspicious, Mary ran off and was sheltered at an inn near the bridge called the Angel. The authorities soon caught up with her, however. After a murder trial in Oxford she was hanged on 6th April, 1752. Her Scottish lover fled to Flanders where he died that December – of arsenic poisoning.

The Angel

Henley-on-Thames

Come in the first week of July to experience the atmosphere of the annual Henley Royal Regatta. This is rowing's equivalent of a Lord's Test, Wimbledon or Royal Ascot. It is a major sporting event, but also an opportunity for ladies to display the latest fashions. The rowing fever first gripped Henley when it was the venue for the original Boat Race between Oxford University and Cambridge University in 1829. The annual Regatta began in 1839. Wealth and privilege were its friends from the start. The Royal part of its title appeared in 1861 when Prince Albert became patron. The Original Grand Challenge Cup has been retired and replaced by a replica donated by Harvard University, U.S.A. Crews come from all over the world to compete for it.

Walkers descend on Henley all year round. This is the eastern terminus of the 65 mile Oxfordshire Way, from Bourton-on-the-Water. It links with the Thames Walk at the Angel on the Bridge. The setting is a worthy one. Henley is on a beautiful stretch of the Thames and at the foot of the Chilterns, with their magnificent beech woods. It is an ancient settlement, a tribal town of the Iron Age *Ancalites*.

The name is still Celtic – *Hen* meaning Old, as in Welsh. With the Thames the major trade route, Henley prospered. Primitive road transport also found the local prehistoric tracks useful. The town is particularly rich in Tudor pubs, when its corn markets and malting kilns were thriving. the Civil War visited the place in the 17th century, but there was soon numbers of admirable Regency and Georgian buildings to show how wealthy its citizens were in the 18th century. Mr. Blandy's fortune didn't do him or his daughter much good when she was arrested in the Angel Inn.

The present bridge was built at the end of the 18th century. When the railway came in 1857, Henley was at the end of a branch line, however. There were commuter trains to London, which suited the stockbrokers. The station was (still is) famous for inebriated race goers during Regatta week. Ex-Beatle George Harrison lives here now, while Michael Heseltine retained his seat as Henley's M.P. in 1992.

The Walk

1. Go left up Hart Street, away from Henley Bridge. Pass St. Mary's Church on your right and a plaque marking the birthplace of William Lenthall, Speaker of the Long Parliament (1640-53) on your left. The dentist's on your right is Blandy's house, where Mary poisoned her father. Turn right along Bell Street. Continue past a sub post-office on your left.

2. Turn left up Badgemore Lane. Go right at Mount View and turn left up Crisp Road. Pass Hop Gardens on your left, then Cooper Road on your right. Within 100 yards, just after house No. 71, turn left up a narrow footpath. This soon bears right. Beatle George Harrison's Friar Park estate is on your left. Continue past blackberry bushes to emerge through a kissing gate beside a gate at a bend in a road.

3. Turn right along the road. Pass the drive to Lambridge House on your right. When the road bends right, go straight ahead over a stile in the corner. Follow the public footpath over the golf course. Continue through a glorious beech wood with bluebells in late April/early May.

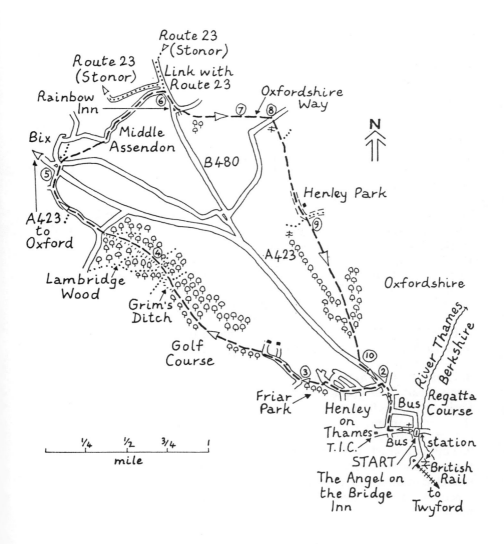

The way-marked path keeps near the edge of the wood on your left, then accompanies Grim's Ditch, an earthwork which could date from the Iron Age.

4. Take the way-marked path No. 48 ahead. Painting the parish path number on trees is particularly useful at a crosspaths, where you go ahead with 48 and ignore 32. emerge at a road junction. Take the road ahead to Bix and the A423.

5. Cross the road carefully and go ahead to the new St. James' Church (Bix used to be on the route of walk 23). Pass this on your left and bear right diagonally over the cricket field to the corner of a lane. Go right and immediately bend left with the lane to follow it to the B480 in Middle Assendon.

6. Turn right to the Rainbow Inn, which is the start of route 23 (Stonor). Link these two routes for a 13 mile walk. Bear left across the road to continue this route by following the Oxfordshire Way into Henley. Turn left and pass Mill Close on your right. Turn right up the signposted Oxfordshire Way. Climb a track with a fence on your left and a hedge on your right. Continue across a field to a gap in a hedge on your left in a corner formed by a fence of a paddock on your right.

7. Bear right to cross a stile in a fence, then a n isolated stile that has lost its fence and reach a stile in the far hedge. This gives access to a lane.

8. Cross the lane to follow the signposted Oxfordshire Way along a firm track ahead. Pass Pond Cottage on your right at its start and pass Henley Park on your left at its end. Go through a gate. The lane bends left, but this route continues through a kissing gate beside a fieldgate ahead.

9. Follow a track with pigsties behind the fence on your left. Continue through another kissing gate beside a fieldgate to cross parkland. Pass a tree-clad mound on your right as you descend to a kissing gate in the fence ahead. Go down a woodland path which leads to a fenced access to the A423 road.

10. Turn left along the A423's pavement into Henley, soon passing 'The Old White Horse' on your left. Pass Badgemore Lane on your right and retrace your steps to the Angel on the Bridge.

27. Mapledurham

Route: The Ferry Boat Inn, Whitchurch – Mapledurham – Holly Copse – Path Hill – Whitchurch Hill – The Ferry Boat Inn, Whitchurch.

Distance: 8 miles.

Map: O.S. Pathfinder 1172 Reading.

Start: The Ferry Boat Inn, Whitchurch (Grid Reference SU 636771).

Access: Take the train to Pangbourne (on the line between Oxford and Reading). Cross the Thames by a toll bridge (free for pedestrians). There are car parks for patrons at both the Ferry Boat Inn and the Greyhound Inn, Whitchurch. You can also reach Pangbourne on the No. 5 bus between Oxford and Reading on weekdays only.

The Ferry Boat Inn, Whitchurch (0734 842161)

Good food is served here, as well as Morland s real ale. Bed and breakfast is available. The bar is open from 11.30 am to 2.30 pm and 6.30 pm to 11 pm between Mondays and Fridays, 11.30 am to 3 pm and 6.30 pm to 11 pm on Saturdays and 12 noon to 3 pm and 7 pm to 10.30 pm on Sundays.

The Greyhound Inn, Whitchurch (0734 842160)

The ferry owner started this pub in the early 19th century. Real ale and bar snacks are served. Opening hours are 11 am to 2.30 pm and 6 pm to 11pm on weekdays, 12 noon to 2.30 pm and 7 pm to 10.30 pm on Sundays.

Mapledurham

Come on a weekend or a Bank Holiday Monday between Easter Sunday and the end of September to visit Mapledurham House. It is only open in the afternoon (2 – 5 pm). The working watermill (where you can buy wholemeal flour) is open from noon to 5 pm and can be visited on Sunday afternoons (2 – 4 pm) during the rest of the year. Combined admission tickets are available to both mill and house.

Mapledurham House is an excellent example of an Elizabethan mansion, being built in 1588. It has remained within the Blount family who settled here in 1490. Their forebear had come over with William the Conqueror and a Sir Walter Blount died a valiant death as the standard bearer in Shakespeare's 'Henry IV, part I'. The BBC based their serialisation of 'The Forsyte Saga' here. Kenneth Grahame (who ended his days at Pangbourne) may have had it in mind when writing about Toad Hall. E. H. Shepard's delightful illustrations for 'The Wind in the Willows' were based on this stretch of the Thames. The Blounts were Roman Catholics and the Anglican St. Margaret's Church is unusual in that its south aisle has been turned into a separate Roman Catholic chapel. The watermill dates from the 15th century, but there was a mill

The waterwheel, Mapledurham

here when the Domesday Book was written. It is reputedly the last working watermill beside the River Thames.

The Walk

1. With your back to the Ferry Boat Inn, go right up the road through Whitchurch, soon passing the Greyhound Inn on your right. Turn right along Hardwick Road.

2. When the road turns left, go straight ahead through iron gates to follow the private road but public path towards Hardwick House. Pass this Tudor house (modernised after being damaged in the Civil War) on your right and continue along a track through a second set of iron gates. Reach a road and turn right to visit Mapledurham House.

3. Retrace your steps along the road to pass the signposted bridleway which brought you from Whitchurch on your left. Follow the road until it bends right.

4. Go ahead up a concrete farm access lane signposted as a public bridleway to Goring Heath. Pass Bottom Farm and a row of cottages. Ignore a stile on your right, go ahead along the edge of a field past trees on your left. Continue beside a fence on your left to a gate in the corner giving access to Bottom Wood.

5. Enter Bottom Wood and follow the path ahead. This soon forks left, as way-marked by a white arrow on a tree. Go right at the next fork which is for a drier, parallel, path. Reach a path junction in the centre of the wood. Bear right, as directed by a white arrow on a tree. Follow the clear path. Pass a thatched cottage on your right, then a house on your left (Holly Copse). Go up its access lane and reach a crosstracks.

6. Turn left along a broad track. Ignore a signposted bridleway to Mapledurham on your left. Go ahead to reach Keepers Cottage on your left. Turn left immediately after it. Go down a track, through a gate and follow a hedge on your right. Cross a stile on your right to go around the edge of woodland on your left. Continue over a stile in the bottom corner. Veer very slightly right to cross a stile in a lower fence and walk with a fence on your right up to a stile in the top corner. Follow a path through a belt of trees to a lane. Turn right past Path Hill Farm Cottage to join a road where it bends.

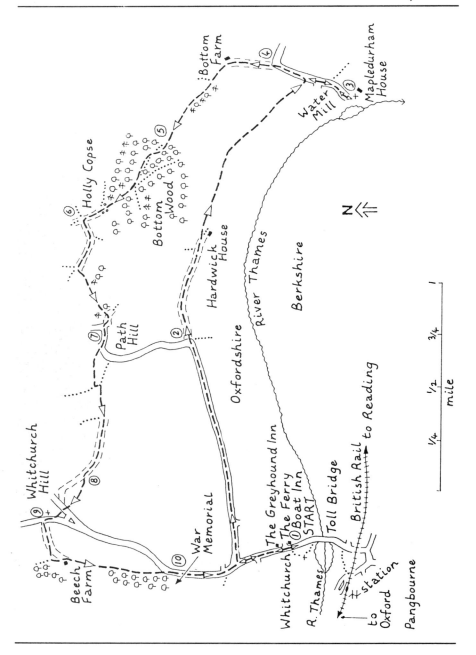

The Ferryboat Inn

7. Turn left to pass Pilgrim Cottage and Path Hill House on your right. Pass cottages and bear right along an enclosed path, leaving the road to bend left downhill. Continue over a stile to enter a field. Walk beside a hedge on your right to a stile in the next corner. Turn left down a fenced track for 50 yards, then turn right over a stile to walk beside a hedge on your left. Continue over a stile to the right of a gate in the next corner. Walk with a fence on your right and past pigsties on your left.

8. Bear left through a kissing gate to take a well-trodden fieldpath. This leads over a stile in a dividing fence to a kissing gate and an enclosed path to a road. Cross this and the village green. Go right at the next road to pass the Church of St. John the Baptist on your right.

9. Turn left up a concrete farm access lane. Reach a gate across it and bear right along a public footpath through a kissing gate. Follow a hedge on your right to a kissing gate used by a path from the wood on your right. Turn left to follow a fence on your right. Go ahead through a gate, cross the access lane and pass Beech Farm on your right. Take the kissing gate ahead. Follow the fenced track which continues through another kissing gate to pass woodland on your right. Go right when you reach a road.

10. Pass a war memorial and cross the road carefully to follow an elevated footpath into Whitchurch. Go down the road through the village back to the pubs.

Sample the delights of country pubs, and enjoy some of the finest walks with our expanding range of 'real ale' books:

PUB WALKS IN THE PEAK DISTRICT
– Les Lumsdon and Martin Smith

MORE PUB WALKS IN THE PEAK DISTRICT –
Les Lumsdon and Martin Smith

PUB WALKS IN LANCASHIRE – Neil Coates

PUB WALKS IN THE PENNINES
– Les Lumsdon and Colin Speakman

PUB WALKS IN THE LAKE DISTRICT – Neil Coates

PUB WALKS IN THE YORKSHIRE DALES – Clive Price

PUB WALKS IN THE COTSWOLDS – Laurence Main

HEREFORDSHIRE WALKS – REAL ALE AND CIDER COUNTRY
– Les Lumsdon

PUB WALKS IN CHESHIRE – Jen Darling

– all 'Pub Walks' books are just £6.95 each

There are even more books for outdoor people in our catalogue, including:

EAST CHESHIRE WALKS – Graham Beech

WEST CHESHIRE WALKS – Jen Darling

WEST PENNINE WALKS – Mike Cresswell

NEWARK AND SHERWOOD RAMBLES – Malcolm McKenzie

RAMBLES AROUND MANCHESTER – Mike Cresswell

WESTERN LAKELAND RAMBLES – Gordon Brown

WELSH WALKS: Dolgellau and the Cambrian Coast
– Laurence Main

OFF-BEAT CYCLING IN THE PEAK DISTRICT – Clive Smith

THE GREATER MANCHESTER BOUNDARY WALK –
Graham Phythian

THE THIRLMERE WAY – Tim Cappelli

THE MARCHES WAY – Les Lumsdon

– all £5.95 except where indicated

We also publish:

Guidebooks for local towns

A guide to the pubs of 'Old Lancashire'

Spooky stories

Myths and Legends

Football books

**and, under our Sigma Press banner,
over 100 computer books!**

All of our books are available from your local bookshop.

In case of difficulty, or to obtain our complete catalogue, please contact:

**Sigma Leisure,
1 South Oak Lane,
Wilmslow, Cheshire SK9 6AR**

Phone: 0625 - 531035 Fax: 0625 - 536800

**ACCESS and VISA orders welcome – call our friendly sales staff or use
our 24 hour Answerphone service!**

**Most orders are despatched on the day we receive your order – you
could be enjoying our walks in just a couple of days.**

An Invitation

Sigma Leisure is expanding and always on the lookout for new books, and of course, new authors to write them!

Our current range includes:

❑ An extensive range of rambling books

❑ Our very popular range of "Pub Walks"

❑ Town & Village guides to the North West

❑ Local history and folklore

❑ Activity interests including Mountain Biking and Football

Future publications include:

❑ Advanced Driving

❑ 'Days Out' for families with small children

❑ Authentic pubs

We plan to develop into other areas very soon, with a focus on sport, entertainment, and many other leisure actvities.

Our speed of production and successful marketing could make a great success of your book. So if you are interested, and have an idea for a book for the leisure market, then why not telephone us for further information or alternatively, write to us at our office:

Sigma Leisure
1 South Oak Lane, Wilmslow, Cheshire, SK9 6AR
Tel: 0625 531035   Fax: (0625) 536800